Straddling the 'HOUND

151 Howe Street, Victoria BC
Canada V8V 4K5

Straddling The 'HOUND
ISBN 978-1-927755-47-1 (paperback)
ISBN 978-1-927755-48-8 (ebook)
Cataloguing information available from
Library and Archives Canada.

Printed on acid-free paper.

Agio Publishing House is a socially-
responsible enterprise, measuring success on
a triple-bottom-line basis

10 9 8 7 6 5 4 3 2 1.1

Straddling the 'HOUND
The Curious Charms of Long-Distance Bus Travel

TREVOR WATSON

Agio
PUBLISHING HOUSE

DEDICATION

To Carl Eric Wickman (1887–1954) of Hibbing, Minnesota.
As a young man he failed as an iron-ore miner and Hupmobile
salesman. Undeterred, he went on, at the age of 40, to found the
glorious *Greyhound Corporation*.

ACKNOWLEDGEMENTS

Many thanks to my publishers Bruce and Marsha Batchelor
of Agio Publishing for their understanding,
great help and unflagging good-humo(u)r.

TABLE OF CONTENTS

PART ONE

To Weed and Beyond

'll start by saying this: I have always been entranced by the idea of travel. I love the idea of looking around the world, looking it up and down, inside and out. Often I have felt I wanted to woo the world, to wrestle it to the ground, to romance it, to know it intimately, break it into little pieces and suck out its marrow.

When I was a little boy there was a world map on my wall – a 'Full-Color Mercator Projection' it was. I can remember wondering what it would be like to sail, say, between Celebes and Borneo, stopping here and there along the way to meet the locals. I'd heard the area was thick with pirates and I'd worked out a rough plan for dealing with them. The plan involved much derring-do on my part, leading to an uninterrupted series of victories. I found the idea thrilling, and still do.

My motive for travel is basically an inquiry into how people in different places view life: how they conduct their own lives, what they think about, what they consider worth spending their lives upon. What do we have in common with one another, and what might I encounter that is alien or shocking? After forty years as a physician, I've never lost my sense of wonder in the human heart and mind; it's an interest that continues to grow.

John Steinbeck wrote that whatever this travel-affliction is, it is altogether incurable. He spoke of "the ancient shudder, the dry mouth and vacant eye, and how four hoarse blasts of a ship's whistle still raise the hair on my neck and set my feet to tapping."

It is a lust, a longing, a hunger, a thirst, an addiction, a yearning, a calling, an obsession, a compulsion, a demanding appetite that howls to be appeased. All attempts at appeasement have, so far, proved futile.

When I was a young adult, my parents – neither of which was so afflicted – said that my passion for travel was something that "had to be simply got out of your system." When the urge comes on me now, it seems reasonable to plan a dozen journeys in a row, and breezily assume they could all be pulled off without a hitch. Really, though, that's like attempting to eat a dozen meals in rapid succession – basically nuts.

In another sense, the love of travel is like the love of music. I have met a few people who are not moved by music, just as I've met people who don't understand the appeal of travel – they'd rather "stay put." To my mind, you can no more get the travel bug out of your system by traveling, than you can get song out of your heart by singing.

Naturally, there's a word, derived from the Greek, for this overwhelming love of travel: it is *hodophilia*: love of the path or road. It would be a great name for a travel company. You've got to love those Greeks.

In a lifetime of travel of one kind and another, it occurred to me some months ago that I had not taken a long *bus* trip for ages. It took me a while to remember just how long it had been. In fact, it was the summer of 1969, when I was 22, a journey from Athens to London. The ticket cost $35, a complete give-away, I remember thinking. It was an incredible test of endurance – sitting up all the time – and I arrived in London feeling deathly ill. I think it was the ice in the glass of milk I drank in a bar in Calais while waiting for the Hovercraft. Or it may have been the *ersatz* orange juice I bought from a vending machine on the Autobahn outside Munich. My stomach reels at the memory.

When I began this book I was 64, and had lost none of my zest for exploring new places and asking nosy questions of perfect strangers. I didn't know a thing about long-distance bus travel in North America, so I did some investigating. I learned that a good way to proceed is to buy a 'Discovery Pass' from the storied Greyhound Bus Lines Incorporation of Dallas, Texas. I decided a 15-day pass would be about right and went ahead and ordered one. For days I watched the mail closely, like when I was a kid waiting for something for which I had 'saved-up, and sent-away.'

I asked a number of friends and relatives if they'd like to accompany me. The typical response was, "Eeeee-ew, are you kidding? Didn't you hear about that crazy guy on the Greyhound who decapitated his seat-mate a couple years ago – ate some of him, too? Not me!"

I had indeed heard the story. It's true and horrific beyond imagining. In the summer of 2008, near Portage LaPrairie, Manitoba, a carnival worker named Tim McLean was on his way home on the bus and was murdered in the most gruesome manner by Vince Weiguang, computer engineer and undiagnosed paranoid schizophrenic.

However, such experiences must occur less than once in a lifetime, so I thought it would be a pretty safe bet to enter the Greyhound netherworld. Nevertheless, I resolved not to be at a loss if I got into a tight spot, and equipped myself with a Victorinox Swisstool, a shrieking electronic alarm, pepper spray and a rapier-like steel walking stick. Let any aspiring decapitator beware of meddling with me. In any case, this was my thinking on the subject at the time.

Accordingly, I set out on a dark and rainy Thursday morning, the 9th of February, 2012. I felt a bit keyed-up, like a fellow who had decided to go sky-diving and was having serious second thoughts. I live near Victoria, BC, so my wife drove me to the ferry terminal near Sidney. Bless her heart, she was delighted for me to be undertaking an unusual project. Besides, she was probably glad to get me out of the house for a couple of weeks. On the ferry I could catch a bus and proceed smoothly to the Vancouver bus station, on Main Street.

I was surprised to find security personnel scrutinizing the bags of the departing passengers. I wondered how thorough these chaps were going to be, because the defensive items mentioned above were expressly forbidden according to a pamphlet entitled *Greyhound Security Precautions*. Through the motions they went, with appropriate facial expressions, grave and suspicious. However, in spite of all their frowning, rummaging, huffing and puffing I somehow got through their screening process with everything intact – every single thing – right under their noses. It was a wonderful example of mock-thoroughness. I was off to a good start.

In due course we crossed the border at Blaine, Washington. I had never crossed the Canadian-U.S. border in a bus before. We were frog-marched by armed officers into the Customs and Immigration hall and asked the usual intrusive questions. From their tone and demeanor I was half-expecting to be herded into a confined space, shaved and deloused under arc lamps.

Of all things, the officers were most interested in how much cash over $10,000 any of us might be carrying. Among Greyhound passengers, I'll bet this has never happened in recorded history, but still they keep looking. I idly wondered what the protocol was if they were so fortunate as to catch anyone trying to bring in such a bale of cash. Would they delay the whole bus? How could you ever catch up to your traveling companions? Maybe I'll try it with *Monopoly* money sometime, just to see how they handle the situation.

As part of the routine these officers x-rayed our bags. One bag after another went in and out of the machine… nothing was turning up. They'd almost finished with us and were looking pretty glum. Then they came to the backpack of the girl ahead of me. Suddenly they perked up – something must be afoot. They had indeed discovered something: firm radiological evidence of contraband. In actual fact, it was an apple… a solitary, ordinary apple… but it was clearly the event of the day for them.

Naturally, they confiscated it on the spot. The poor girl herself was trembling at this point, and I suppose she was hastily preparing some kind of defense in her mind. In the end, however, she was not charged, but escaped with only a warning, stern and official. I wondered if the officers filed a report on this offense, or whether they discussed the case over beer after work, or with their wives at home in the evening. You couldn't pay me enough to do that job.

As we buzzed down I-5 toward Seattle, it occurred to me how carefree this type of travel is. No worries about driving, navigation, mileage, mechanical problems, or fatigue. Why, you could chat to your neighbor, sleep, eat, read, and plan your next move, all while sailing down the highway, seated comfortably upon leather, at seventy miles an hour – for pennies a mile. How much easier could travel be?

I figured if I had taken full advantage of the pass, I could cover about 1000 miles a day for $23 – one of the true travel bargains of all time. You don't even have to find a hotel... you can just keep on rolling all night if you want. You can clean up at a truck-stop in the morning, and get a couple of toothpicks to prop your eyes open.

I like those big colored printed sheets they give you in coffee shops along the way. They're called *The Coffee News*... local ads and events, horoscopes, jokes, famous quotations and a quiz. I found the following on my first day. The originator of the statement was not given, but it strikes me as wonderfully true:

> *The privilege to work is a gift,*
> *The ability to work is a blessing,*
> *The love of work is success.*

As night fell we approached Seattle. As we went through Everett I saw off to my right, on a dark and rain-swept corner, an old-fashioned red neon sign saying simply: *TOYS ... OPEN.* It seemed particularly melancholy to me... some little toy vendor, Mr. Bill Widgett, as I imagine him, sitting alone in his shop, working late, perhaps dusting the toys, talking to them, stewing vaguely about Toys 'R' Us... holding on by his fingernails, trying to scratch out a living that dismal winter night, hoping a customer might come in.

Eventually we made it to Seattle, where I needed to transfer to another coach. I took a look around at the people in the terminal. A very rough-looking lot, to be sure, the motliest-looking assortment I'd ever seen in my life. Most looked like convicts being transferred from one penal institution to another. These people looked like the extras in *The Shawshank Redemption*. I checked my pepper-spray; I switched off the safety.

One chap particularly caught my eye; he was as stocky as can be; his neck must have been 20 inches around. He was, I imagined, Carlos "Chopper" Ramirez, out on weekend parole. He had cryptic messages tattooed on his neck and bald scalp. His head actually seemed suffused, as though it was about to explode. Oddly enough, he had – of all things – a huge golden *polo* medal hanging around his neck. I'll bet you anything it was stolen, or maybe won in a knife fight.

I had chosen Olympia, the state capital, as my stop for the first night. The condition of the bus depot was utterly deplorable. For one thing, it was locked – indeed padlocked – from the outside, like a shed. There was a huge sign, in blue and white, with the letters B-U-S arranged vertically, like children's blocks. The B was burnt out; the U was flickering; the S was fine. The effect was rather disquieting.

I disembarked, and got my bags from the cargo hold. There I was, standing alone in a strange city on a rainy winter night, not knowing quite what to do. I was expecting a taxi to be easily available, but there was none to be seen all up and down the rainy street. I noticed a seedy convenience store down the way and I made my way toward it.

In I walked, shaking my umbrella. I approached the middle-aged Chinese woman at the till. She was watching a video. She looked bored, but appeared annoyed to be disturbed.

"Say," I said cheerily, "I just got off the bus and need to call a taxi. Can you suggest someone I might call?"

She looked up and scowled; she evidently disliked the riff-raff that drifts over from the Greyhound station – mostly shoplifters and drug dealers, in her books. She said not a word, but pointed to a phone book across the store. I called a company called Capital Cab; I asked to be picked up at the Greyhound depot. I thought I heard the dispatcher laugh as I hung up.

I walked back to the depot, studying the shadows, juggling my bags and umbrella. When I arrived there was actually a cab waiting, but not the one I'd called. The driver was Ray, a lean, friendly man of about 65. Of course he offered me a lift, but I decided to wait for the Capital man. He was there in a minute. I started to feel as though things just might work out, after all. At least I was out of the weather.

In the light of the next day, the Olympia bus station was not quite so foreboding as it was the night before, and a lot more interesting. The woman at the ticket counter, I suspect, had a number of endocrine issues.

She asked, "What do you want?"

I explained with a touch of pride, that I had a pass, in fact a *Discovery Pass* – as if I was likely a charter member of the *Platinum Elite Greyhound Society*.

She was evidently quite unimpressed.

I sat down, a bit crestfallen, and awaited events.

A gaunt black man about 60 then came in, hoping to get on the next bus to Denver. He had an enormous black bag.

The woman said, "So what's in the bag, bud?"

He replied that it was a fold-up bicycle.

What ensued was a thoroughly distressing dispute over whether this bag should be treated as luggage, or as a bicycle. Luggage was free; a bike was $45; he had a ticket, but no money for baggage. You see the problem. He had checked with Greyhound on the matter, and they said that it could go as a suitcase – but she wasn't buying it. She said she was "way too busy" to check with head office herself. She enjoyed her authority, throwing that considerable weight around. They were deadlocked.

Then this interesting man – for whom I had much sympathy – pulled out his cell phone and began to call his children in different cities, asking for a little help. He must have called four or five of them, most of whom apparently stonewalled him, for reasons that can be imagined. Eventually he pieced together commitments for the required sum, and arrangements were made to wire the money to Western Union in Olympia by four that afternoon. Throughout, the agent treated him disgracefully, in spite of the fact he was very polite with her. It was a small indication of what it must be like to be poor and black in this society.

At this point I thought it wise to use the facilities, and I tried the door to the *Gents*. It was locked. Unfazed, I approached the battle-axe and asked for the key. From the back room she produced the key attached to a grubby white plastic flyswatter.

I told her I'd nail any flies I happened upon; she was not amused. However, she said that because I was the first one to use the facilities that day, I had to turn on the light. Fair enough, thinks I. She then proceeded to give me detailed directions as to how to find the switch in the dark.

"Right in front of you is a wall, see," she said. "You reach around the left end of the wall, see, and there's a switch. That's the light switch." She gave the directions slowly as though she were a long-suffering teacher, and I her slowest pupil.

As we pulled out of the Olympia depot my eye was caught by an establishment across the street, where, come to think of it, I might have stayed the previous night, had I known of it. It was the Olympia Inn, and its sign boasted, among other alluring features, *FREE TV*. This was clearly a cutting-edge sort of place. Another feature of this spruce place were the numbered plywood diamonds in various faded colors affixed to the doors. Really sharp.

The scenery along the highway south of there was soggy and dull. Everything seemed the same color, an amalgam of green, grey, brown and black. It was the kind of prospect that makes you want to look away.

It was then I noticed an interesting passenger ahead of me on the left. He was a giant of a guy with a full grey beard and for reasons unclear to me, he was wearing red plaid pajama-bottoms. He had a half-smoked cigarette behind his right ear and appeared to be mumbling to himself, and grinding his teeth. Could this be another highway headhunter? Not a bit; I later learned that he was an injured commercial fisherman, who was just in from the Aleutian Islands the day before.

My thoughts were diverted by a woman behind me talking at the top of her voice on the phone. She was talking to the parole officer of her lover-boy who had recently failed to show up for a court-mandated appointment. He was thought to have possibly absconded, which I thought was pretty much a sure bet. The woman – I reckoned her name was Shawneeza – was quite agitated. She let it slip – silly girl – that he had "lit out for North Carolina," and wasn't planning to come back anytime soon.

"I need him to come back," she said. "Besides, the kids need shoes." I pictured him on an east-bound Greyhound at that very minute, on the outskirts of Omaha, with a big smile on his face.

The driver of this particular bus was a remarkably rude piece of work. When I showed him my pass, he snatched – and I *do* mean snatched – it from my hand and demanded, "Where you goin,' man?" "Well, I never...!"

He never wasted an opportunity to be rude to a customer; I was watching how they reacted, reading their faces. It was as though Rule #1 for this lad was to alienate as many passengers as humanly possible in the time available. He was almost like a caricature of a rude person, like the 'Soup Nazi' on *Seinfeld*. I think of him as the 'Bus Nazi.'

Because this bus was new and had Wi-Fi, I sent an e-mail to Greyhound head office describing my dismay concerning the conduct of the driver of bus #86317. My guess is that my complaint got automatically deleted somewhere in the ether. I considered slipping the man a note, but I thought that might make him... *snap*. He'd have swerved into the oncoming lane, or perhaps over the nearest cliff. It would have served us right.

And speaking of WiFi: Greyhound offers *Free WiFi* on selected buses and routes. I rode on many buses that claimed to have this feature, however, most were entirely free of WiFi.

In Eugene, Oregon a disabled woman of about 45 got on the bus. She had a service dog with her, a Siberian Husky. The driver very reluctantly made adjustments to accommodate them, grumbling all the while. I spoke to this woman and discovered that she was epileptic. The dog had been trained to detect a subtle change in breath-odor, which signaled an immanent seizure. The dog would raise the alarm, the woman would take an extra dose of her anti-convulsant, and the seizure would be averted. Very neat indeed; I'd never seen such a thing before. The dog's name was Max, a lovely fella.

We were about to get on the road again when it became obvious that the bus wouldn't go into gear. After perhaps thirty attempts, the driver arose and began to leave the bus.

A passenger called out, "Is everything OK with the bus?"

He snarled, "No, everything is not *OK with the bus!*" With that he stormed out. Out of the corner of my eye, I think I saw him kick a tire.

After about half an hour in limbo, the word went out that we were to be sent a "rescue bus" from some distant place. Now I know a sinking ship when I see one. It was mid-afternoon and I decided that rather than waiting to be rescued, and then travel late into the night, I might as well grab a motel and start fresh in the morning. The other passengers – one of whom was a dead-ringer for Charles Laughton in *The Hunchback of Notre Dame* – did not have this option. They had to use their tickets on the next available bus. So off I went into the rain in a Eugene Budget Taxi, a shiny orange minivan. The driver was an intelligent and articulate man by the name of Gary; we chatted the whole time, mostly about motorcycles, with which I have had a life-long love affair.

Later that evening I shuffled across the parking lot to Denny's and ordered one of their "skillet dinners." It turned out to be a perfectly delicious melange of chicken, broccoli, potatoes, sour cream and onions. It was the closest thing to *home cookin'* that I'd had for days – two, precisely, but it seemed much longer than that.

In the morning I called Budget again and in a few minutes came a heavy knock on my door that made me jump... such service! The Budget man was a stubby and swarthy hombre originally from El Salvador, he told me. He carried my bag to his car – which was a budget rig, for sure. It was a twenty-year-old faded heap of a Crown Victoria, just about a goner. The steering wheel cover, originally cheap and dreadful, was worn to the extent that what had once been leatherette was dirty foam rubber. Never mind, this was just the vehicle to get you into the right head-space for riding the 'hound.

The word budget, incidentally, is derived from the Latin word *bulga*, meaning a small leather bag, and is related in some obscure way to the word belly. It forms an odd juxtaposition with Taxi.

A very pleasant chap he was, too, the patriarch of a multitude, he told me. Until six years ago he was a roofer, but a serious fall cut short that career. He landed on bark mulch, otherwise he would have been killed, he said. Being a cabbie provided enough income for him to make occasional trips to the old country. He'd recently been there for two months and had had a great time. However, he said, there were about 15 murders a day in his city, although he'd seen nothing himself.

I wandered around downtown Eugene to pass the time before the bus left. An interesting business caught my eye. It was, in fact, The David Minor Theater and Pub. I'm not quite sure how it works, but the marquee showed that there are four shows a day, and I imagine you can get a beer and a meal while you sit in the dark on comfy chairs and watch the movie. Seems like a wonderful idea to me – an idea whose time may have come. Sure beats watching all the anonymous sports in the ordinary pub, or eating goopy popcorn in an ordinary cinema.

At the appointed time the bus pulled out. Today's driver was a stickler for the rules, and hence I thought of him as 'Reg.' He read us the amplified version of the entire Greyhound constitution, I think: all about alcohol, drugs, profanity, cell phone etiquette, musical devices and breaking wind. He followed up with the one about having to wear shirts and shoes ("for sanitary reasons"). Strangely, he omitted any mention of pants; I guess he gave us some credit.

"And remember," he said, smiling into the mike, "they're cell phones, not yell phones." I liked that one.

A word about the Greyhound dress code: the men and boys all wore basically the same outfit, almost as if it were a uniform: dark-colored hoodie, jeans and running shoes. Most of the fellows who looked like pillars of the Greyhound community also wore what Canadians call toques, pronounced 'too-kes,' and what are called 'stocking-caps' in the U.S. The way the women dressed was unremarkable, and certainly not as stereotyped as the men. In terms of men's grooming, I would say this: if you really want to fit in, wear a greasy mullet and a scraggly beard.

Another observation: almost all the riders – including the driver – were smokers. These people were clearly pretty hard-up, many unemployed, but boy, could they smoke! At one stop, Reg, a smoker himself, announced, "No smoking this side of the Coke machine." He made up rules as he went.

If smoking were permitted on the bus it would be suicidal just to be there. If I were a politician and asked what I intended to do about poverty, banning tobacco would be a major plank in my platform. On average, I reckon, it's $150 a month up in smoke, plus, of course, resulting medical costs. Getting the votes of these guys, however, would be a hard sell.

We soon passed Roseburg, where I'd intended to spend the previous night. I was attracted to the name of the town. In reality, it appeared a scruffy and dismal place. I'm an inveterate reader of signs as I travel;

many are amusing to me. Roseburg offered several signs that caught my eye, so it was not a dead loss. A shop, barely standing by the look of it, was called The Other Hand. Then there was the Pepsi sign with M-O-T-E-L hand-lettered on the bottom half. It makes me shiver to even think of spending a night in the place. It reminded me somehow of the Bates Motel in *Psycho*.

Just down the road was a huge billboard advertising the local Casino that had signed Herman's Hermits to perform at a date in the near future. I remember this group from when I was in high school in the sixties. I liked their simple ditties just fine. Judging from the billboard, lead singer Peter Noone hadn't changed so much as a hair in 45 years, and his teeth were whiter than ever – blindingly white, rather like stumps of chalk.

Onward we rolled, to Grant's Pass in southern Oregon. I saw a sign there which is as bad a business name as one could choose: *Lawless Roofing*. Pardon me, but I believe I'd be more comfortable dealing with another firm altogether, preferably a zealous respecter of the laws of physics, especially those concerning gravity and osmosis.

Somewhere near there I saw another business, this one engaged in the art of the tattoo. Now I have seen enough tattoos to last me several lifetimes, and I confess, I don't know what on earth the appeal is. Upon inquiry I discovered some historical details about what seems to me a lamentable practice.

The word *tattoo* is derived from the Samoan *tatau*. The first written reference to the word itself appears in the journal of Joseph Banks, the naturalist aboard Captain Cook's ship HMS *Endeavour* in 1769: "I shall now mention the way they mark themselves indelibly, each of them is so marked by their humour or disposition."

Later I learned that the island of Great Britain takes its name from tattooing. *Britons* according to one account means 'people of the design,' and the *Picts* – meaning 'painted people' – from the north of that island were famously tattooed blue. Even today, Brits are the most-tattooed people in Europe. I love knowing stuff like that.

The history of tattooing is fascinating. Forcible tattooing was done as identification in Nazi concentration camps. Roman soldiers were required by law to have identifying tattoos on their hands in order to make it difficult to hide if they deserted. Gladiators and slaves were likewise tattooed; exported slaves were tattooed with the words *tax paid* and it was a common practice to tattoo *Stop me, I'm a runaway* on their foreheads.

As Robbie Burns said, "Man's inhumanity to man makes countless thousands mourn." More like millions, at this point.

Emperor Constantine banned tattooing the face around AD 330 and the Second Council of Nicae banned all body markings as a pagan practice in AD 787. The Latin word for *tattoo*, interestingly enough, is *stigma*.

Tattoos seem to correlate to certain other unfortunate phenomena such as incarceration, drug abuse, single motherhood, probation and drunk-driving convictions. Tattoos are also apparently related to the economic necessity of traveling by bus. On my way today I saw a tattoo parlour called *Nukklheadz*, which seems to me a wonderful piece of self-parody.

Enough about tattoos! I hope never to think of them again.

Today I noticed there was hardly any conversation on the bus. It appears that about 90% of passengers are traveling alone. Most spend a great part of their time plugged into headphones, presumably listening to music. I actually found this discouraging and somewhat annoying. When your seat-mate has his earphones in, he's sending you a pretty clear message. My guess is that a lot of these people have pasts they're not keen to divulge to strangers, especially nosy ones like me.

My across-the-aisle neighbor was a seemingly untroubled soul. He had been eating junk food all day. Discarded wrappers surrounded him. He was a headphone guy; his head bobbed sleepily. I wondered what tune he was listening to. About four in the afternoon he opened up an interesting product – candy, I guess – called *All Fired Up*. He kept on bobbing his head. His incendiary snack seemed not to be firing his brain a bit.

Most of the talking you hear comes from someone on a cell phone. It usually goes like this: "Honey? I'll be at the depot at six… OK… yup, chicken's fine… I love you, Honey… bye."

By late afternoon, Mt. Shasta came into view off to the north, through the windows on the right side of the bus. There it was, the most splendid sight: a gorgeous white giant thrusting itself into the bluest sky you ever saw. Steam trailed from its peak. At 14,179 feet, it is the second tallest volcano in the Cascade Range. *Shasta* is derived from Russian, the language of early settlers in the area. It suggests: 'white, clean, pure' or 'happiness, luck, fortune, felicity.' I'll wager they liked it here a good deal better than the Steppes.

This struck me as just the place to stop for a night or two. The nearest bus stop was in Weed, in Siskiyou County. The name of the place itself excited my curiosity. When planning this trip, I learned that the town has about 3,000 residents and was named after lumber baron Abner Weed. He founded the town because the winds were good for drying lumber.

The bus depot was a most modest affair, even among bus depots. It was, in fact, a log cabin with a flat roof perhaps a bit larger than a garage. A few of us got off the bus and shambled into the hopelessly cramped structure. The only touch of modernity was a small electric sign in the window saying *Open*. I learned that the place opens only when a bus is expected – not the sort of business that would support its owner in much style. The proprietor put on the coffee in anticipation: 75 cents a cup.

When I reached the counter I asked the beefy female agent, "Where's the Motel 6?"

She answered, raising her nose in a northerly direction, "Oh, it's a long way off – maybe 3 miles."

I said, "Well I guess I'll be needing a taxi."

"Ain't none," came the reply. Her mind was clearly elsewhere.

Now I subsequently found out that Weed itself has shops, restaurants, motels, a mayor and council, a college, brewery, a drunk-tank, law courts, police and fire departments – but curiously, not a single taxi. A curious omission, to be sure, and a hot moonlighting opportunity for the Greyhound staff, between buses.

There was nothing for it but to walk – I figured an hour. I really didn't mind: the weather was fine and I'd been sitting on my duff all day. I remember walking three miles along a highway when I was a boy and found it quite tiring. In reality, the motel was scarcely a mile away and I had just warmed to my task, when to my delight, I arrived. There it was – that big, friendly red, white and blue sign. I could hear Tom Bodett: "We'll leave the light on for ya."

One thing about Motel 6 is that the rooms are all identical, wherever you go, so it's like arriving home at the end of the day. Call me crazy if you will, but that's how I feel about it.

Later, just before dark, I went for a walk around town. The part along Historic Highway 97 is rather unremarkable, but if you go into the old part of town, under the newly refurbished iron archway with W-E-E-D welded to the top, things began to look a lot more interesting. I plunged in and soon encountered a dog that didn't seem to like the look of me. He looked a little like Old Yeller, just before they put him out of his misery. I fingered the pepper spray, but decided against it. I simply changed course slightly, avoiding any unpleasantness.

The downtown buildings were old, but well-built of brick. You could tell the place had once been prosperous, but the prosperity appeared to have moved on down the line. These buildings housed a few starving businesses, closed for the day – or perhaps for the duration. I read somewhere that "taxable sales within the city are somewhat limited." I passed a forlorn flickering sign announcing the availability of *Cocktails*. Above the sign, against the darkening sky, was a depiction in red neon of a martini, complete with olive and swizzle stick. The idea of spending 'happy hour' there gave me the jimjams.

Across the street from the cocktail lounge stood a building that looked like a disused art-deco movie theatre. Near its front door was a poster under which was printed *Now Playing*. The movie was, and I swear it's true, *Attack of the 50-Foot Woman*. It showed a woman standing astride a highway overpass filled with cars. She had long wavy hair and a heaving, creamy bosom. Her dress was hiked up. She was picking up cars and tossing them around with impunity, while tiny men in fedoras looked on fretfully. She looked more like a fifty-yard woman to me.

I later learned that this is indeed a real movie, a sci-fi outing released in 1958, directed by Nathan H. Juran, no less. It stars no one I'd ever heard of. One reviewer fondly called it a "bad film of incredible notoriety" – a "proto-feminist cult film" – whatever that may mean. *Rotten Tomatoes* gave it a score of 75%, while commenting that, although it was one of the worst sci-fi movies ever made, that didn't prevent it from being 'thoroughly enjoyable.' And to think, had I not gone to Weed, I probably never would have learned any of this. I began to feel a bit giddy, as if I was in a rather pleasant episode of *The Twilight Zone*.

I continued to walk toward the end of the town. There I found an enormous building, a warehouse originally, I think. The immense sign announced this was, in fact, *The Weed Mercantile Center*. A beautiful mural stretched along the wall facing the town depicting a wonderful old steam locomotive pulling rail-cars laden with enormous logs – redwoods, likely.

The only other person about was a woman of slight build, about 70. She was wearing black earmuffs and smoked a very long cigarette, perhaps a Virginia Slim.

She looked me up and down, smiled, and asked, "Out for a walk, are you?" She didn't say, but I believe her name might have been Blanche.

I briefly told her that I'd read a bit about Weed, and the place interested me, mostly because it was near Mt. Shasta. "Are you local?" I asked.

"Yup. Sixty-two years... right here," she said.

We chatted a bit longer and then parted pleasantly.

On the way back to the motel half an hour later, I stopped in at Ray's Superette to see what I might get for supper, for I had decided to 'dine-in.' I cruised the aisles and to my surprise, rounded a corner and ran smack into Blanche, still in her earmuffs, apparently considering the purchase of a bottle or two of wine. We recognized one another and said hello a bit awkwardly, and I carried on. I later met her at the cashier and I was pretty sure by that time she was starting to think of me as "that weirdo drifter that come into town on the Greyhound... Up to no good, likely... maybe I should call Sheriff Pickens. Better safe than sorry."

The cashier was a young black woman with the astonishing name of Markeshia, according to the tag on her apron. I learned somewhere that the parents of each black daughter in the U.S. try to give her a name different from any other black girl born in that year. I have no idea how this information is administered, but the system seems to be working. The name Markeshia may be unique in history, for all I know.

The most interesting establishment on Main St. had a catchy name: it was the Hi-Lo Restaurant Motel & RV Park. An antique neon sign – all swirls of red, green, yellow and blue – glowed magnificently in the dark. The place fairly dripped nostalgia. The sign noted that the Hi-Lo had been *Serving Friends Since 1951*. Perfect.

I peered in through the misty window into the rosy glow and saw throngs of happy diners chowing-down. Above, mounted heads of deer, moose and bobcat looked on glassily. I walked in, feeling completely

alien, but enjoying it immensely. Country & Western music was playing, something about crying, lying, cheating and dying. I asked to see
the menu. The waitress was most obliging.

"Sure, honey," she drawled; she didn't bat an eye.

The menu featured real stick-to-the-ribs fare. I decided I'd return
for breakfast.

Back I went to the Hi-Lo in the morning and had a truly memorable
feed of hot Italian sausage, scrambled eggs, hash browns and buttered
sourdough toast and jam. Thus fortified, I thought I'd attend a church
service, but from one end of the town to the other, I found no evidence
of one, which I found disappointing and surprising.

I opted instead for a walk out to the College of the Siskiyous, on
the east side of town. There I found an enormous deserted campus – not
a soul around – with decent-looking, dark-stained, low-rise wooden
buildings. I wandered over to the track and first-rate grandstand and
sat on a cold aluminum bleacher reading Taylor Caldwell's *Great Lion
of God* for a while. I was feeling a bit lonely at this point, for the first
time since I left home.

The College of the Siskiyous describes itself as "one of the most
beautiful campuses in the state... established in 1957... publicly-fund-
ed community college... classes began in 1959 with 67 students...
now 4,000... excellence in firefighting, nursing, music..." and so on.

My view is that this college in Weed is so isolated, and the town
itself so lacking in diversion, there's precious little else to do but study.
On special occasions you could, of course, head to the Hi-Lo for the
Blue-Plate Special, or maybe catch *The 50-Foot Woman* again.

I had brought a minimum of baggage with me – 'travellin' light' –
for once in my life. The problem with that is that you have to seek out
laundry services fairly often. Therefore, when I saw the washer and
dryer at the motel, I went to assess the situation – costs and so on. To
my considerable surprise and pleasure, I learned that cleanliness was
on offer for 75 cents a pop.

The other part of this is that you have to decide how to carry this out without exciting a charge what my old Dad called 'indecent exposure.' I'm pretty sure they lock you up for that in Weed. This is one way of doing the laundry when you only have one outfit: completely undress... then don your bathing suit and windbreaker... proceed to the laundry and get the washer going. Then return to your room for a breather. Half an hour later, you return to the laundry, pop the wet clothes into the dryer, and retire to your room once again. So far, so good. When you imagine your load is dry, retrieve your clothes in a plastic bag, return to the room, and put them on. The pleasure of donning clean, hot clothes is better than a trip to a spa – and all for $1.50.

The only snag with all of this was that the dryer was a bit harsh. In fact I noticed my barely-broken-in Tilley hat had a nasty rip in it across the front. Well, I don't mind traveling by bus, but I do draw the line when it comes to wearing ragged clothing. Therefore, I decided I needed to repair this damage forthwith.

When you're alone in a motel room in a forgotten town at night, you have plenty of time to solve problems as they arise. I proceeded thus: I whisked down to Ray's again and bought some adhesive tape, a packet of 40 needles and thread. I returned to the motel and fashioned a very neat and inconspicuous patch for my beloved Tilley. Thus, my respectability was restored for a mere $2.14.

I learned that they brew good beer in Weed, and I decided it would be a shame to leave town without trying some. At seven o'clock I wandered over to the Hi-Lo and ordered a bottle of Abner Weed's Amber Ale. It went down very smoothly. I then proceeded to devour their Seniors' Turkey Dinner, which was delicious in all respects, a complete gastronomic bull's eye.

Another fact or two about the Weed Brewery may be in order. Their product is known as 'The Legal Weed.' Apparently the owner of the brewery had been in a protracted dispute with the federal government – the Department of Alcohol, Tobacco and Firearms, to be precise – about making so bold as to call beer *weed*. I believe he won the lawsuit, a triumph of wit over bureaucracy. Another of the brewery's witticisms is, "A friend in Weed is a friend indeed."

Weed... what a fun town.

As you might imagine, the shops along the main drag were replete with souvenirs positively exhausting all the plays-on-words of *weed*. Numberless T-Shirts, mugs, pencils, erasers, key chains, flashlights, shot-glasses, hats, rabbits' feet, kaleidoscopes and do-dads with something like, *I LOVE WEED* emblazoned upon them. I wonder what old Abner would have thought. I reckon he'd have been delighted.

Next day was Monday. It was time I was pushing off south again. The bus was scheduled to depart at 0800. My alarm went off at 0545. It took me fully 45 minutes of hard work to get out the door and aim myself toward the Hi-Lo. It was a dark trudge; snow was falling at weird angles – just so it hit any exposed skin. I put up my umbrella. I wondered if the bus was going to make it through the snow. In any case, the Hi-Lo was warm and cheery and had only a few customers – locals, for sure at that hour. I was feeling a bit rushed, so I just ordered a ham and cheese omelette, spelled *omelet*. And what an enormous creation it was: roughly the size of a pillow, and packed with miles of cheese and what appeared to be the major parts of an adult pig.

After bolting this huge thing, I loosened my belt and got on my way. I hustled up the hill towards the depot. It was snowing harder than ever and I had a headwind. It reminded me of a picture I had seen in a Frank Netter anatomy drawing in medical school of a fellow who had just eaten in a restaurant, and went out into a blizzard with two suitcases. It showed him turning blue, in the process of having a heart attack.

After a thoroughly bracing walk, and with rosy cheeks, I stumbled into the little depot. I was the only customer. The coffee was on; I wondered if it was fresh or left over from the midnight bus. The proprietor was a phlegmatic soul, and testy to the point argumentativeness. The kind of guy who if you said "good morning" to him, would retort, "What's so good about it?" I'll call him 'Bud.' After my eyes adjusted to the dim interior, I saw a huge dog lying just behind him. This was Rudy, and he was a Rottweiler. It's interesting what breed of dog a certain person chooses. A Rottweiler was a perfect choice for Bud. The funny thing was that Rudy's personality was all pussycat. Rudy and I hit it off just fine, much to Bud's disgust.

On my heels was a young fellow in his early thirties, small, wiry and pleasant-looking. He said he had followed my tracks in the snow. King Wenceslas flashed through my mind. He said he was trying to get home to his mother's place. He was unable to get a job and needed to take refuge for a while. I asked him what he ordinarily did, and I gathered he was good at working on complicated small machines. His last job was assembling machine guns for a 'businessman' who imported them from Eastern Europe.

"Not much of a market for them these days," he said sadly.

I wondered if he had a letter of reference from his former employer in his pocket. Such a reference might do him more harm than good.

Moreover, this fellow had a serious problem using his right thumb, which pretty much disqualified him from his customary work. He said he couldn't afford the required investigation and treatment. This struck me as tragic and uncivilized. He couldn't work because he was disabled and he couldn't get treated because he couldn't earn enough to pay the exorbitant medical bills. Therefore, he was going home to mother. In any other first-world country this would not be happening. Still, he was a cheerful lad – Scott was his name – and we talked on and off all that day.

Next to come in, in a whirl of snow, was a vivacious, extroverted woman named Katherine. She was about sixty and was, I learned, a semi-retired high-school teacher from Dixon, west of Sacramento. "It used to be spelled D-i-c-k-s-o-n," she noted.

She wore an elastic brace on her right wrist. I displayed some professional curiosity about the wrist injury, somehow letting it slip that I was a physician. Well, did that ever put a fire under the conversation! Pretty soon we had a bustling out-patient clinic on the go in the Weed Greyhound depot. Bud was keen to show me his war wounds.

"See this one here, Doc?" pointing to a dint on the left side of his skull. That's from 'Nam in '68," said Bud. "The Tet Offensive… Hell on wheels."

This, to me, pretty much excused his sourness.

It seems that Katherine's husband's great-grandfather was John Muir (1838–1914), one of the patron saints of the environmental movement, an early advocate of wilderness preservation and founder of the Sierra Club. Katherine noted tartly that she thought old John would disapprove of most of the political positions of the Sierra Club today.

The bus was an hour and a half late getting in, what with all the putting-on and taking-off of chains. The chains are of course applied to the drive wheels, which are actually forward of the rear-most wheels on these buses, something that was news to me. Again, the arriving passengers looked a deprived, furtive lot. I had heard that California has been releasing loads of convicts, more for reasons of overcrowding than good behavior, unless I miss my guess.

Actually, of course, they were nothing of the sort. They were in fact a multiracial group of high-spirited folk in toques, hoodies and backwards baseball caps – smokers all, full of quips and raucous mirth. Bud wished us god-speed.

So long, Weed. I was missing it already.

Scott, Katherine and I sat near enough to one another on the bus that we could converse. The subject of baggage arose. People pay lip service to 'traveling light'; certainly most of us do nothing of the kind. Katherine said the best number of socks to take with you on a trip is three. I'd always thought of socks as existing in pairs, but not so, this clever woman. "Sure," she said seriously, "you wash one sock each evening, dry it overnight, and then put it on in the morning. That way, your socks are pretty clean all the time. I asked her if she thought the socks should match one another. Somewhat desirable, she suggested, but not strictly necessary. In fact, if they don't match it's easier to keep track of what sock to wash, when. She struck me as a no-nonsense pioneer kind of girl, the kind that comprised the backbone of the Old West.

Two seats ahead of me on the right was a man who kept turning in our direction and tossing out the odd comment with a smile. I moved forward so we could talk. He told us his name was Hans and he was the son of an American Jewess and a Mennonite from Switzerland. On the bus there's no telling who you'll find. He informed us that he was, in fact, a Messianic Jew, which seemed entirely in keeping with his family background.

He told us he was making a pilgrimage to Bethel Church in Redding, just a few miles south of where we were. He was an ex-soldier, a veteran of campaigns in Vietnam and El Salvador. He mentioned that he was disabled with PTSD, and the VA was very slack in looking after his medical and financial needs. Moreover, he'd had two hip replacements, several cardiac stents put in and had recently suffered a stroke affecting his short-term memory. He was going to Bethel Church to seek divine healing – something that happens frequently there, he told us.

At this point Katherine joined the conversation. She was a Catholic, she said. Her background was Irish, her maiden name was Kilkenny. Hans said the previous year he'd had a near-death experience that took him to the gates of Hell, which scared him out of his wits and had affected him profoundly thereafter. Katherine said she didn't believe in Hell but quickly added she thought Hell was 'here,' pointing out the window. The scene outside was lovely, all forest, sky and snowy mountains.

I said that I thought Northern California was far too attractive to really be Hell. She fell silent. I asked her if she thought her disbelief in Hell really determined if there was such a place or not. I'm told some people don't believe Idaho exists. That doesn't change the fact that there it sits, large as life, in a neat slot between Washington and Montana.

I added that if she calls herself Catholic, the teachings of Christ need to be held in high esteem, and certainly He believed in the existence of Hell. She continued to furrow her brow – likely wishing it was time to get off the bus. As we neared Redding we decided we'd pray for Hans. The three of us joined hands and did just that.

This man radiated joy in spite of his afflictions; I really took to him. When we parted in Redding, he said, "See you later," and raised his eyes and smiled.

I was sad to see him go, but very much warmed by having met him. Altogether a marvelous day so far, and it was only lunchtime.

We got a new driver in Redding, one Karl Jones, according to his lapel badge. He looked and spoke for all the world like Rush Limbaugh. This thought kept me amused throughout the tedious announcements. I had hoped to make it to Madera that night, but we arrived in Sacramento an hour and a half too late for my transfer. Never mind, I thought, I'll spend the night here and set out fresh in the morning. I called the Motel 6 just down the street and, learning it was a mere ten-minute walk, set out directly.

While I was preparing to cross an intersection, I heard someone come up behind me and say my name. I jumped a bit and then saw my new friend, Scott, and his seat-mate, Richard, approaching me from behind. We were all headed in the same direction, and I was glad to have their company because the neighborhood was pretty rough, and seemed to exude an electric edginess. I got the distinct impression that I had better keep my wits about me. Richard had a very scarred face and I suspect some brain damage. I thought he must be ex-military.

He said, "We've got your back!"

I found the expression comforting, and immediately felt perfectly safe there. They said they were, "Goin' for a beer."

I carried on and checked in. At the desk I was greeted by a huge, unfriendly black man. His attitude was something in the line of, "What do *you* want?" He assigned me a room, and I asked him if I was on the quiet side of the building, which had but two sides, one of which faced the freeway. "One of 'em," he said cryptically.

As I walked to my room I passed a young black couple standing by the pool. It was the off-season, and the pool was empty and deserted. He was about 25 and she 16, I figured. He caught my eye and asked, "How are you, sir?"

I said I was well, thank you.

Encouraged by my responsiveness, he smiled at me and asked, "How's the trip going, anyway?"

I felt a growing unease that was somehow intensified by the fact he had a gold canine tooth that glinted in the late afternoon sun. I was pretty sure what all this friendliness was about, and I gave the young couple a miss. They must have attracted some business shortly thereafter, for when I drew back my curtain ten minutes later, they were gone.

The Internet at the hotel was 'down' and against my better judgment, I decided to walk to McDonald's and use their free WiFi. The sun was just about gone; my antennae were straight-up. I looked over my shoulder at the motel as I walked away. Several people, including the man on the front desk, were watching me intently from their windows. The oddest sensation came over me, as though I'd become the target of a conspiracy.

As I walked briskly along armed with my walking stick, imagine my surprise to hear my name again. Sure enough, it was Scott and Richard, fresh from their pursuit of refreshment. I asked them where they had gone.

Scott said, "Oh, we just bought some beers at the 7-11 and drank 'em in the bushes."

This statement surely illustrates the flexibility and thrift of a true Greyhounder. I was proud of them. It was coming time for them to get their bus and I walked them back to the depot and said good-bye to them – for the third time.

When I reached McDonald's I looked up at their sign and got an update on how many burgers they had sold so far. Now, I don't know who tallies them all up, but so help me, the sign said 85 billion. I started to fantasize about all this meat. Let's see... at two ounces a patty, that works out to be 10,625,000,000 pounds of beef.

Thought of another way, supposing you can get 500 pounds of hamburger from each critter, you'd need 21,250,000 cows, steers or bulls to pull this off, a sizable herd, to be sure. You might be inclined to think that this must be all the beef there *is,* but you'd be wrong. At last count there are something over a billion and a half cattle in the world, mostly in India.

Alternatively, if you put these burgers side by side, they'd reach a distance of 5,500,000 miles: that's 233 times around the world. If stacked, allowing for an average thickness of 3/8 inches, they'd reach a height of 100,000 Mount Everests. I am, however, on the verge of a digression.

A little later I bought a pint of milk at the nearest convenience store. On the way back in the dark I had to walk through a gloomy underpass. I could see out the other end and did not realize until partway through that in the middle of it was an enormous black fellow in a black hoodie. Naturally, all I could see were the whites of his eyes. Though tingling with excitement, I didn't break my stride and uneventfully made it back to the room with my milk.

I used some of it on my cereal and placed the rest on the cold pavement outside my door. When some time later I went to get more of it, I noted with some alarm that the milk had been moved. It now sat, about eight feet away, on top of the air conditioner. I retrieved it with some suspicion and found that it was full. I took no steps to determine what fluid now filled my milk carton, but it takes little imagination. I just left it there. It's hard to explain, but in the entire trip I only experienced the approach of what felt was *evil* once – and this was it.

That night I put a bunch of furniture against the door and engaged my burglar alarm. I was preparing to retire at about 10:30 when there came a great pounding on my door.

"Waddya want?" I growled, trying my best to sound fierce. I didn't look through the peep-hole… that's a good way to get shot in the eye, I'm told. In any case I assumed malign intent, but it may just have been a pizza-delivery fellow with the wrong room number, who knows?

There was no response.

All in all, it was a very interesting day, and I slept like a top.

The next morning I called my old friend, Jan, in Bakersfield. This is a man I'd met in Israel a few years ago who asked me to look him up if I was ever in his area. He is a surgeon. He was most gracious and insisted that I stay with him for a few days. I agreed to spend that night at his place and he said he'd pick me up at the depot that evening.

It was a relatively quiet day as we bussed through Stockton, Modesto, Madera, Fresno, Visalia, Porterville, and finally reached Bakersfield at about five. I was fumbling with my phone, trying to call my friend, when I heard my name being shouted. Sure enough, it was Jan. He had parked just out front, and soon we were in his car, ready to go. I saw him slip something into the glove compartment. I don't know why, but I asked him what it was.

"Oh, that," he said, "that's just my nine-millimeter Glock. I'd never go into a Greyhound terminal without one."

He lived 25 miles west of town in the foothills of the Sierra Nevada Mountains – a place called Hart Flat. This is the exact place described in *The Grapes of Wrath* that the Okies fetched-up, looking for work. The place the migrant workers camped is today a vast expanse of tawny grassland. Jan noted that this was a 'very conservative area,' which is code meaning that the locals hate the President, own lots of guns and have a year's supply of food in their bunkers.

The homes were scattered over a huge area. Each homeowner had perhaps 15 acres separating him from his neighbor. Maybe it was the mood I was in, but there seemed a distinct feeling of unhappiness and paranoia in that affluent but strangely unappealing neighborhood.

One of the drawbacks of 'democracy' in the U.S. is that most people don't seem to approve of the man or party in power – "I never voted for him, never would." Most people who say they are in favor of democracy usually disapprove of the outcome of the process. It's an illustration of what Churchill said about it: "Democracy is the worst form of government except all the rest that have been tried." My feeling is that the average person is, in effect, in favor of a dictatorship – with himself doing the dictating. I get a big kick out of human nature.

My friend, his wife and I spent a very quiet and pleasant evening together. He said he had to be in the operating room at seven the following morning, so we had an early night.

I was up at quarter to six and soon ready to go. I waited in the living room for a long time. All was quiet. All at once… instant pandemonium erupted. My friend had been 'on call' all night and had accidentally switched off his alarm clock. In due course, he awoke naturally, saw the time and panicked.

There was no time for breakfast; out the door we ran. We zoomed back to Bakersfield with the wheels of his Prius barely touching the ground. We averaged 80 mph and treated each stop sign and red light with disdain, as if we were an ambulance. He was torn as to whether to go straight to the hospital, or to drop me at the Greyhound. He was already late for the surgery and noted, "I get charged $60 for each minute I'm late!" What a system!

However, hospitality trumped the hospital and he took me to the bus station, near a store called The Wooden Nickel. The name of the place made me smile; it reminded me of my old Dad who always told me not to take any of those, no matter what. I bought breakfast in the station from a large radiant black woman that called each customer (including me), "Dear." That simple word really warmed my heart. It's hard to explain, but it was what the Bible calls 'a word in season.' I was alone, a long way from home, heading into the unknown and it made me feel just right, and I told her so. I bought more than I intended to, just to make her happy.

Someone asked her what kind of day she was having and she smiled and said, "Why, my day has been just one blessing after another." I was glad to be in the same room as she was.

Well, I needed to meet my buddy Wally in San Diego that night, so I figured I'd better get on with it. There are two buses from Bakersfield to San Diego, one requiring a transfer in LA, one not. I figured I might avoid bloodshed or other inconvenience in LA if I took the latter. My choice of bus that morning proved more important that I had imagined. I'm not sure how the folks on the other bus made out, but the experience on our bus that day was completely unpredictable – wonderful in spots – and ended up by making this day the most eventful and interesting of the whole trip.

What I didn't know is that the bus I so cleverly selected was not Greyhound at all, but one of the seedy Crucero fleet, bound for the Mesa Central de Autobuses in Tijuana. In the last few years, Tijuana has become a leading center in the principles and practice of decapitation… sacks of heads, all over the place, I was told. I imagine all this mayhem keeps loads of people busy matching individual heads with their original bodies. I found myself wondering if they found a particular head and not the body, the funeral would require a very small casket indeed.

The bus was shabby, and pretty much packed. There were the usual garden-variety Greyhounders, plus what looked like a few migrant farm workers, clutching Walmart bags, munching tortillas, heading home. I found an empty seat on the aisle about half-way along the left side of the bus. By the window sat a large man of about 45.

"OK if I sit here?" I asked.

He nodded slightly. I took the seat.

After a minute or two of silence, I asked, "Where you headed?" I thought this was a reasonable attempt at conversation… friendly-like, not too nosy.

"Ell-ay," came the reply. Period… that was it. No further information, no question, nothing. The conversation I'd hoped for was still-born; my heart sank. I reckoned it was going to be a long, quiet ride; I fished the novel out of my pack and began to read. I became aware of widespread coughing. There must have been about six passengers hacking at any given time. I squirmed a little… TB? Valley Fever? Mold?

I smelled the strong scent of tobacco coming from behind me. I turned around to see from whom this emanated, and I was startled to see a Buddhist monk gazing serenely out the window, complete with shaved head and saffron robe. There's absolutely no telling who your fellow-travelers will be on the bus.

After about twenty minutes of this, I noticed my seat-mate started showing some signs of life. "Did you hear that 'pop' sound?" he asked.

I hadn't.

"Blowout," he said.

The bus pulled over and drew to a stop on the shoulder. I remember thinking I was glad we were not in a plane. The flustered little Mexican driver went to investigate. The tires were inflated, although pretty much worn-out. He decided he'd better check the engine compartment. Many of the passengers got out to take a look; several had opinions on what might be wrong. Most of the chatter was in Spanish. After a minute or two the driver determined that a spring clip had failed on the high-pressure hose to the turbocharger. He said, "I got no tools!"

I thought the fact that he was unprepared for the most elementary mechanical repair entirely in character with this outfit. I truly believe that the corporate maintenance policy for these big bus lines is to drive their rigs to death, or at least until they break down at the roadside.

This, if you're counting, makes two breakdowns since leaving home a week before.

I felt for my Swisstool – which, of course, according to regs I ought not to have had on my person – and offered it to the driver. He fiddled around for quite a while, practically standing on his head in the engine compartment. There were many grunts and Spanish expletives. After he was clearly out of ideas, and with skinned knuckles, he gave us bystander-advisers an odd smile and a shrug of his shoulders. We were, as we say at home, *hooped*.

Throughout, we got the distinct impression that the driver did not want to seek professional mechanical assistance, even though we were actually at a truck stop with full repair facilities. It was as though any repair costs would be deducted from his pay, or perhaps he would get sacked for breaking the bus.

Somewhere in there I chatted briefly with the monk, who was a world-class cigarette smoker when the system permitted, such as during mechanical breakdowns. He was from Thailand, and lived in a monastery in Los Angeles. I tried some Thai phrases on him, for example, "Hong nam u-tinoi?" ("Where's the toilet?") He smiled inscrutably, and exhaled in my face. I later saw him catching a ride from a trucker who'd stopped for fuel. His serenity and patience evidently did not extend so far as to waiting for our rescue bus to arrive.

Eventually, and after much discussion, head-scratching, calling head-office and the like, it was decided to consult a mechanic. On cue, a mechanic mysteriously emerged from the shadows, like he was expecting to be called upon. He was a tall, slim man, with a far-away look in his eyes, a man I thought we could count on. He looked a bit like a rider of the range – like Clint Eastwood in *High Plains Drifter*, come to think of it; I could imagine him twirling a box-wrench like a six-gun.

The upshot of the foregoing was that a part was required and, sadly, unavailable at that time and place. Moreover, the mechanic insisted that the vehicle was definitely unsafe to operate – much too slow for the freeway on which we had been traveling.

Decision-making is an interesting and unpredictable process in this type of situation. After listening to the mechanic carefully, and nodding sagely, our little driver, flying in the face of expert counsel, ordered us back on the bus. He had decided to take us back to Bakersfield. He was, you might say, prepared to *wing* it.

We moved along the shoulder at a snail's pace. I didn't mind; I was kind of having fun at this point, and everyone was talking and joking about the ridiculous turn of events. I used my GPS to determine our speed. At first it was 30, flat-out; then it was 27, then 21. I imagined we were in a plane losing altitude, hoping to clear that range of mountains ahead.

Through all this, my seat-mate had been free with his opinions, and not the taciturn type I had originally taken him for. He was, in fact, a long-haul trucker who'd lost his license "for impaired" some years before, so he felt qualified to advise us on all matters concerning the road. He said there are loads of accidents on that freeway where slow-moving vehicles get clobbered from behind by enormous trucks operated by wide-eyed drivers on *bennies*.

This information introduced a strain of considerable anxiety among those within earshot. Just behind us sat a black woman who listened carefully. She was about 40, six feet tall, very well turned-out, mostly in red. Suddenly, she sprang to her feet and bolted to the front of the bus. This is getting interesting, I thought. Then in a voice that would have raised the dead ten miles away she bellowed, "You, drivah! You stop dis bus right now 'n' call fo' anudder one! Eee-mediately, o' I's gonna sue yo' ass!"

The effect was electrifying on all of us, especially the poor driver, who by that time had likely decided on a career change. By some odd chance we were just feet away from another truck stop, namely, Bear Mountain Plaza – not a bear or mountain anywhere near there, by all appearances. In any case, #60544, flagship of the mighty Crucero fleet, sailed limply into port.

We soon learned that a rescue bus had been dispatched from Los Angeles and was expected in a couple of hours. I spent the intervening time wandering about the place chatting to the staff, reading, checking the merchandise. The maintenance man in the restaurant was a fine fellow, with a warm smile and good eye-contact. He was taking a break and drinking from a thermos with the inscription *The Lord has promised good to me* on it, which rang a bell with me. I thought it might be from Psalms, but it's not. In fact, it is from John Newton's *Amazing Grace*:

> *The Lord has promised good to me...*
> *His word my hope secures.*
> *He will my shield and portion be as long as life endures.*

In due course our rescue bus arrived, just about as decrepit as the one we were abandoning. The two vehicles looked like litter-mates. There were laughs all around as we piled in. I sat with the same lad I'd been with earlier. For some reason, he seemed eager to tell me a good deal about himself. I'll call him Alonzo Ruiz. As I mentioned, he was a long haul trucker, the type of vehicle known as a 'semi,' or 'tractor-trailer.' He told me he'd lost his license 'for impaired' almost three years before.

This is how it happened, most unfairly, of course – to hear him tell it. It seems he was out on the road somewhere with his cargo, and decided he needed a break. Up ahead was a casino, one of hundreds that line the highways of North America. Alonzo, it seems, was not averse to a bit of gambling, and he was feeling thirsty as well as tired. Well, one thing led to another, and he eventually emerged from the casino several hours later pretty sozzled. Shocked at how late it was getting, he decided he'd better stay in the casino parking lot for the night. To avoid the bright lights he thought he'd better move his rig to a far corner of the lot. And, what kind of rotten luck do you think tripped him up? Just as he was driving a mere stone's-throw, down swoops a Highway Patrolman with a Breathalyser machine.

Well, he was good and busted at that point. The three-year license suspension suggested that this may not have been his first offense, but I didn't press the point. I asked him how he supported his family these days. Apparently he has a brother who is a carpenter near San Francisco and he had found some work with him. He noted that his wife was a manager at a Mexican supermarket in Riverside, and somehow they kept afloat. He said it would only be another month and he'd be back on the job in earnest. "Easy to get a trucking job," he said, "but the pay sucks. Awful competitive, and you're always in a hurry. Still, I'm happy to be going back."

Ahead of us to the west stood the Sierra Nevada; this range of mountains is known as 'The Grapevine' to long-haul truckers in that area. As we labored up the eastern slopes, I noticed quite a number of emergency runaway lanes. Alonzo said truck brakes fail 'all the time,' and these lanes are in constant use in that area; and he would know.

In a while we approached what looked like a strange factory, a dismal, dusty emplacement, set way off to the right of the highway. I thought it might have been a nuclear power plant, or a place for recycling tires, but Alonzo said, "Oh, that? That's San Quentin."

I straightened up in my seat; who doesn't have ideas about San Quentin? It ranks way up there with Alcatraz.

I saw lots of black-and-white movies when I was a kid about San Quentin; they all had to do with the activities of its charming and ingenious inmates: fist-fights, riots, fake guns carved out of soap, squirming through ventilation shafts or sewage pipes, and home-made knives they called shivs. By the way, *shiv* is from the Gypsy word *chivomengro*, any sharp or pointed implement used as a weapon. Jailbreaks were, of course, the main thing on the minds of these lads – many were planned and attempted, though very few realized. A tiny hope is all you've got at San Quentin, I guess.

I later learned that San Quentin Penitentiary is, in fact, many miles away, in Marin County, on the ocean near San Francisco. In any case, it gave me a chance to think a bit about the prison system in California. In the most recent year for which I could find figures, there were 170,000 inmates in adult prisons in California. This is a rate of incarceration is about one in every two hundred state residents.

The California Department of Corrections and Rehabilitation has been much in the news lately because of the terrible crowding of its prisons – many over official capacity. This has led to many early – some would say *unwise* – releases. I'm not sure how the convicts are actually selected for release under these circumstances; maybe there's a lottery system, or perhaps they play *Monopoly* and can actually redeem the *Get Out of Jail Free* cards. If the state builds more prisons in future, will these early parolees be called back inside to finish up? Perhaps they discharge the lucky ones with a few bucks and a Greyhound ticket out-of-state.

We rolled along, down the western slopes. Somehow, the subject of toilet paper came up. Toilet paper is seldom thought-of, except when there is none to be had. It then becomes of paramount importance, more than the economy, more than climate change, more than radical Islam. A fellow across from me said when he found himself in need, he would use one of his own socks. He didn't say what he did with it afterward. It's clear to me that if you 'go Greyhound' enough, sooner or later, you'll have opportunity to talk about anything the human mind can conceive.

In many countries, especially in Asia, you are expected to provide your own toilet paper. In North America, people have grown accustomed to having it provided by the management. The quality of free toilet paper in the US is excellent, pretty much as good as you'd have at home. I remember once being on the biffy at the British Museum, and noticing that each wee rectangle of crinkly, shiny paper was imprinted *Property of Her Majesty's Government*. I'm not sure if Her Majesty actually knew about this, but if she had been informed, I'm sure she would not have been amused. For her sake, I hoped the toilet paper at Buckingham Palace was a good deal less harsh. I believe the practice of embossing the toilet paper in government WCs has since been discontinued. Maybe the ink was allergenic.

According to my sources, the first outfit to mass-produce toilet paper in the New World was the Perforated Wrapping Paper Company of Albany, N.Y. This company apparently had quite a line, among them: *Wrapping, Waxed, Anti-Rust and Carbolated Papers.* In an 1886 ad the company promised that by using this wonderful stuff 'Physicians' and Plumbers' bills' would become a things of the past. Moreover, 'Clogged Pipes with Consequent Impure Air and Disease' would be banished forever. And what a deal! A roll of 1000 sheets could be had, *Wrapped Securely in Tin Foil*, for fifty cents, postpaid. A medicated product, claimed to prevent hemorrhoids and other itches was available for a modest additional charge.

In due course we rolled into Greater Los Angeles. Alonzo directed my attention to the scene on the left side of the coach. There it was, up on a slope, the HOLLYWOOD sign that I'd seen so many times in films. The letters are somewhat out of line, like they had been placed by a crew of dopers. More likely, the poor alignment is due to tectonic shifting because the hillside sits upon the Pacific Ring of Fire. I read there are something like 10,000 earthquakes in LA in a year. Los Angelinos apparently take these things in stride, but it must desensitize people and affect the local mentality a good deal, like living at the foot of Mount Vesuvius.

Incidentally, the sign was erected in 1923, and built to last 18 months. It is comprised of letters 50 feet high and 30 feet wide and originally spelled *Hollywoodland*, the name of the swanky housing development there. Sadly, in the summer of 1932 an unemployed 24-year-old starlet named Peg Entwistle threw herself off the *H* in a fit of despondency over being unemployed. The day following her suicide, a job offer arrived in the mail.

About sundown we rolled into the LA Greyhound depot. I understood this bus would stop here for a short time, then shove off for San Diego – no need to transfer. I felt like stretching my legs and checking out the L.A. Greyhound depot, which I figured was bound to be chaotic and colorful. I stepped down onto the platform, and what do I see on the luggage trolley? My very own pack that someone had unloaded from the baggage compartment under the bus. "What's this?" I thought. "This is supposed to stay aboard, because this bus is going to San Diego."

I immediately seized the bag and dragged it inside the bus, resting it on my lap, thinking of how fortunate I was to have spotted Greyhound's error. Several minutes passed, and it began to dawn on me that I was the only one on the bus, and it was entirely dark inside and out. I sprang to my feet with a sense of alarm and rushed to the front, where I found the little driver, after the most stressful day, doing paperwork by flashlight. I asked him what was going on. His eyes grew wide and he exclaimed, "Oh, Sen-yor, you need to be on the other bus, the one that's just leaving."

Well, I fairly flew out of the old bus onto my new one. I thought I had all my belongings, but to my dismay I soon realized that I'd left my wonderful, enormous novel aboard the old bus. I hope it fell into appreciative hands.

The episode of being on a dark, empty bus reminds me of those stories you hear about some airline passenger who is allegedly asleep when the plane lands and, to her horror, awakens hours later, still in her seat, in a darkened hangar. These somnolent people – whose stories to me are universally preposterous – normally end up wailing about their emotional trauma to the media. The object, of course, is a fat cash settlement to calm their nerves... the *green poultice*, as we say in my line.

I briefly wondered, because of my state of upset, if I stood a chance with Greyhound, and decided, no... no point... I wouldn't get a cent.

I imagined I'd get a letter from head office in Dallas advising me to "tell someone who cares."

On we went through the great, dark, sparkling conurbation of coastal southern California known as the Los Angeles-Long Beach-Santa Ana Metropolitan Statistical Area. Recent figures put the population at 15,000,000, which makes it the twelfth largest city on Earth, fitting neatly between Manila and Calcutta, though less than half the size of Tokyo. In any case, it seemed endless. By the way, I'm giving Tokyo a miss.

About nine we arrived at the bus station in San Diego, which is right downtown, at 1313 National Street. I was less than a mile from the hotel where I'd agreed to meet my buddy Wally that night. The streets were well-lit and empty. The prospect of walking seemed safe enough. I'd just shouldered my pack, when to my surprise, my cell phone rang. After a moment of wondering who this could possibly be, I decided it must be Wally.

"Hello, is that you, Wally?"

Well, it wasn't Wally at all – it was my friend Alonzo from earlier that day. In the afternoon I had lent him my phone to call his wife, and now that he was at home in Riverside, he retrieved my number and decided to check up on me.

"Are you OK?" he asked, with what seemed to me real heart. I assured him that I was fine, and planning to hoof it to my hotel, no problem. "Do ya need anything? Is there anything I can do for you?"

I replied that I appreciated his concern, that everything was under control – but if I hit a snag, I'd call him. We rang off. I can't express how touched I was at his taking the trouble to call me. It was a very nice piece of ambassadorship, I thought. Here I was, a lone stranger in a strange land, and he, an LA-Hispanic defrocked long-haul trucker, was thoughtful enough to honestly welcome me to his part of the world. The call lightened my heart; I set off with a bounce in the direction of the Solemar Hotel.

I was, in general, impressed by the humor, generosity and open-heartedness of many of my fellow-travelers. There was a quality of what I might call *rough goodness* in the ones I got to know as we rolled along. I had encountered this feeling before – in the characters of Steinbeck's early novels – *Cannery Row* and *Tortilla Flat*, particularly. It's strange but true that someone you've just met will divulge things to you that he wouldn't tell his wife or close friends.

I moved through the empty streets at good clip, on high-alert. The hotel where we were booked was a swanky spot, oodles of stars, unaccustomed to having guests walking over from the bus depot. I'd been on the road for a week and looked it, I imagine. I had my pack on my back and my patched and stained Tilley on my head. Not wishing to provoke the management, I paused for a moment to see what changes might be in order before I came in view of the liveried doorman.

My pack is a marvel of engineering; it is, to be sure, a *hybrid* piece of luggage called a rolling backpack. As well as the way I was carrying it on my back as I approached the hotel, it has a handle so it can be carried like an ordinary suitcase. But the best part is that it has two wee wheels on it, and a handle for pulling it along. This may not impress you too much, but I can tell you – the front desk hotel staff makes a firm class distinction between a guest who comes in rolling his bag with alacrity, as against one who trudges in with a backpack.

Accordingly, I straightened up: chest out, stomach in, Tilley stowed, rolling my tidy bag. The staff positively lit up to see me.

"Yes, sir," said the night manager. "We have your room ready. Mr. Hasker has already arrived."

Up I went in the gilded elevator feeling as though I'd entered another world. I approached our room. I slipped the card into its slot. Wally was on his bed watching a huge television. We greeted one another enthusiastically.

"Did you have a good trip?" he asked.

I smiled, took a deep breath and began with, "Wait till I tell you…."

PART TWO

The Road to Key West

derive at least half the enjoyment of any journey by reading about it ahead of time. I had originally intended to fly to Orlando and then take the bus north – to St. Augustine, Savannah and Charleston, and had read quite a bit about those places before I left home. However, the bus connections to those places were awkward, so I decided to head south instead.

I was intrigued by the idea of taking a bus to Key West... who does that? Certainly no one I've ever known. I had a slight acquaintance with Key West, in fact I'd been there twice before. I knew something of its reputation as an artistic, libertarian, dissipated, end-of-the-line fleshpot. I was mortified when I realized my last visit was in 1969, fully 43 years earlier. On this basis, the sobering thought occurred to me that this visit surely will be my last.

I left home Tuesday, Oct 30, 2012 and took the ferry across the Salish Sea to the Mainland. Because I had turned 65 the previous June, the ferry was free; it was a pleasant way to start a trip, and likely the only free transport I'd find for a very long time. I spent most of the crossing trying to adjust my mind to being on the road again. It is a heady feeling, like chugging a mug of champagne.

I needed to catch a local bus ticket to the downtown Greyhound terminal, so I approached the uniformed man at the Pacific Coach Lines desk on the 5th deck of the ferry. He was taciturn, to say the least... no pleasantries at all. He was remarkable also for his very stubby fingers – they were downright *pudgy* as though they had no bones in them. Nevertheless, he handled the cash and tickets with great dexterity, like a card shark.

Initially I sat near some girls who were in their late teens. They all fiddled with cell phones and chewed gum. Their chatter was, as far as

I could tell, entirely vacuous, and it was certainly annoying, punctuated here and there by lamentations about money. The words 'like' and 'wud-ever' – with the emphasis on the latter syllable – were sprinkled about with abandon. I decided to move; honestly, I'd sooner have been in the engine room.

Soon thereafter I felt a pang of curmudgeon-guilt, and resolved to do some work on my attitude. When I was a teenager, I'm sure I annoyed more than my share of adults. I remember sitting on a stack of newspapers at a magazine stand reading a magazine for free. I had an army surplus jacket on, and sported a beard. A couple of middle-aged men walked by me and one said to the other, "If I'da done that, my Pappy woulda horsewhipped me!"

In due course I arrived in Vancouver; while waiting for the connecting bus I had a wonderful snoop around Chinatown. In and out of markets I went, seemingly invisible to those around me. I've never met a Chinatown I didn't like – exotic enough to be intriguing and familiar enough to be reasonably comprehensible. At one point I was amazed to see a severed pig's head on a platter. No one else seemed to take the least notice. I guess you get blasé if you see such things every day. For no good reason, I reckoned this pig used to be the feminine of the species – something like *Miss Piggy*. Her eyes were closed and she looked peaceful – if a trifle anemic.

It felt great to be on the loose. At one point as I walked, I was accosted by a haggard-looking woman about forty. She welcomed me to Vancouver, and asked if she could ask me a question. I may have been impolite, but I said she could indeed *not* do so, and I bid her farewell. I'm not sure why I reacted that way, but I suspect it's an example of the maxim, *The confused mind always says no.*

Late that afternoon I boarded the Greyhound in Vancouver. The driver was a small, very polite black man in a blue toque, with an "anything I can do for you" attitude. Was *that* ever different and refreshing! There were only seven passengers. We proceeded smoothly southward.

Smoothly, that is, until we arrived at the border. This was the same place that I mentioned somewhat disparagingly in the last chapter.

At the Customs stop, one of our group, a guy named Steve, who looked like Yo-yo Ma, said he had to run back to Canadian Customs to get his passport. There was a collective furrowing of brows. Quickly, we all put forth theories as to why this might be necessary.

As the story eventually unfolded, it seems that when he entered Canada the day before with a view to visiting his honey, he made a misleading statement to border authorities. Anyway, he was detained for a while, but in a strange mix of sternness and kindness they let him into Canada for 24 hours, but retained his passport as collateral. You can imagine how he felt. He hoofed it north a couple of hundred yards and took care of business.

Well, Steve's business with the Canadian Customs held us up for at least half an hour. Then he had to pass through U.S. customs – another twenty minutes. Throughout, our little driver, still with toque pulled down over his ears, was the soul of patience, although all this made us seriously late. Clearly in the Greyhound universe you have to be philosophical about these things. Wonderful to behold, the driver's patience was contagious; no one complained, and on we went into the rain and darkness.

When pulling out from every stop our driver read a list of Greyhound commandments to us, as if he were Moses addressing the children of Israel. His manner of reading was really unusual; I've never heard anyone read like that. His meaning was clear enough, but the way he said it was like someone from Mars practicing his English.

"For your com... fort and safe... tee, do... not stick... your... head... out of ... the win... dow." Every time he said it, he did so with the utmost sincerity, and as though he had never done it before. "This bus... is... equip... ped with a rest... room. If... you use... it, please... be care... ful."

In Bellingham, an odd lot got on the bus – they looked like the cast from *The Rocky Horror Picture Show.* Then I realized this was the night before Halloween and these people were getting an early start, maybe going to a celebration somewhere down south. A tall black guy of about sixty got on; his face was sad as a Bassett hound. His hair was in dreadlocks; he wore a natty blue trench-coat with matching hat with big ear lugs and dangling strap. The entire effect was disquieting; I thought vaguely that he might be a warlock or sorcerer. You never know who's boarding the 'hound.

I have often wondered about dreadlocks. I remember asking a young fellow how he managed to have hair like that and he said, "It just goes that way if you don't wash it." Well, I didn't believe it for a second. In my insatiable quest for what my detractors call *trivia*, and having nothing pressing at that moment, I made it my business to inquire into the subject.

Simply put, dreadlocks are matted coils of human hair. I have learned it is possible to promote their development by mercilessly back-combing hair of a certain length. Some claim, however, they get good results by leaving the hair strictly lone; this is called the *neglect* method, otherwise known as the *organic,* or *natural* approach. The thought mildly irritates my inner curmudgeon.

The history of dreadlocks ('locks,' 'dreads,' 'Jata' in Hindi), however, is long and convoluted. However, not wishing to unduly try you, I'll give the briefest outline. In recent decades, dreadlocks are most commonly associated with the Rastafari movement, an African-based spiritual ideology which started in Jamaica in the 1930s, many of whose adherents worship the late Ethiopian Emperor Haile Selasie (1930-74) as the latest incarnation of God. Rastifarians commonly use *cannabis* in their sacramental and sanctifying rites for its 'natural conscious-exalting properties' conducive, so they say, to 'truthfulness and prophecy.'

Dreadlocks also turn up in the histories of north and east African peoples. They have been seen on the statues of ancient Egypt, and on mummies. The Spartans of ancient Greece sported them, as do present-day *Sadhus* in India. In the Old Testament, *Nazirites* – those who consecrated their lives to God as described in the book of Numbers – had hair that looked much like modern dreadlocks. Samson is the best-known Nazirite. Now when I see someone with dreadlocks I think of Samson, and remember how important his hair was to him. This seems to calm that inner curmudgeon.

Next to get on the bus was a beefy fellow in camouflage garb who managed to collide with everybody on the aisle as he made his way to the rear of the bus. He did, however, apologize sincerely as he went, "Sorry, sir… sorry, ma'am."

And then there was the serious young oriental woman with deep pink hair and a polka-dot jump-suit; the effect, I must say, was rather arresting.

I had to somehow get from the Seattle bus depot to the airport, and reckoned it was a long way, so I asked our diminutive driver for advice. I had to get to Westlake station of the Sound Transit Light Link Rail system in order to get to Sea-Tac Airport. He advised me to walk along 9th Street for "oh, 'bout tuna-haff blocks"; he said I couldn't miss it. If there's one certainty in my travel experience, it's if someone says that to me, I'll almost certainly miss it, usually by a considerable margin.

In any case, as I prepared to stomp through the dark, rainy streets of Seattle, I decided to deploy my stout Fulton travel umbrella. When I bought this umbrella, I noted it was manufactured by the firm appointed by Her Majesty Queen Elizabeth II to do so – and I imagine she knows a thing or two about umbrellas. My heart warmed at the thought of the Queen using an umbrella practically the same as mine. I had visions of a footman holding it for her, deflecting rain and wind, preventing, one hopes, a royal respiratory infection – anything from sniffles to pneumonia.

The umbrella is indeed a commonplace item but it is surely one of the unsung bargains of our world. In the UK it's known as a *brolly* or *gamp;* in the U.S. many call it a *bumbershoot.* My mother calls it an *umberdoodle;* my grand-daughter calls it a *bella.*

Consider for a moment what a marvel of utility it is, what a life-enhancing wonder. To my mind, the first thing it provides is a priceless feeling of security when one ventures outdoors. You may stride out of your house with impunity, day or night, secure in the knowledge that you have nothing to fear from weather, man, nor beast. This is no exaggeration.

The umbrella keeps you dry, of course, and thus reasonably warm – all the while protecting you from the nefarious *chill.* My old Grannie was forever warning me about the dire consequences of *catching a chill.* "A nasty chill," she told me, "is nothing to fool with." After decades as a family physician, I still bow to her wisdom.

An umbrella can be used to conceal one's identity if necessary, and perhaps to fend off hooligans, charging animals and such. It has even been used as a weapon of assassination. In 1978 a Bulgarian dissident writer Georgi Markov was killed in London by a dose of ricin injected by an umbrella designed by, we are reliably informed, the KGB.

The umbrella is like a little house, really, when you think of it – a turtle's shell that affords many of life's necessities. Carrying an umbrella with you also means you don't need to lug around a foul-weather suit when you travel. Even on a sunny day the humble umbrella is splendidly useful keeping the sun off. Just think of the cases of melanoma and other skin cancer that might be prevented, not to mention sunstroke.

But – sticking with this slight diversion for a moment – what do we really know about the umbrella? If you're anything like me, precious little, except how to use one. The word itself is from the Latin *umbra,* meaning *shadow.* The suffix *-ella* connotes *small.* Therefore, we may say that *umbrella* means *little shadow.* While I love the etymology involved, it doesn't even hint that you might actually use it in the rain.

There should be a term, derived from Latin or Greek meaning 'nice little portable dry spot.'

Archaeologists tell us that the umbrella has been in use for some 4,000 years. Evidently, the earliest models were made of tree branches covered with big leaves. The Chinese were into the game early, about the eleventh century B.C. Their parasols were covered with paper; later they waxed and lacquered the paper, for water repellency. At various times leather was used; that paragon of inventiveness, Robinson Crusoe, used animal skins. The advent of silk made it possible to make a *foldable* umbrella; the first steel-ribbed umbrella was invented by a Londoner named Samuel Fox in 1852.

Nowadays, most of the world's umbrellas are made in China. In fact, the city of Shangyu in southern China has more than a thousand factories churning these things out. We go through a great number of umbrellas, apparently. In the U.S. alone 33,000,000 umbrellas are sold annually; the largest supplier of umbrellas in the world is Totes Isotoner Corporation, of Cincinnati.

This is likely all the self-respecting person needs to know about umbrellas.

I sloshed along the street for a while, following the bus driver's instructions, until it dawned on me that they must have been riddled with error. Up ahead was a movie theatre with an enormous vertical neon sign that put me in mind of the court of Louis XIV. The many colors reflected in the puddles on the street; I made my way to the ticket booth looking, I imagine, pretty pathetic. The agent, bless his heart, knew exactly where I needed to go. He peered through the foggy glass, and said in a clear voice through the hole, "Sure, it's in the basement of Nordstrom's, just over there."

It was indeed; I was finally getting somewhere. The train ride itself was terrific, conveying me to the airport with marvelous efficiency for the minuscule sum of $2.75.

When I arrived at the rail station at Sea-Tac it was inky dark; I was tired and damp all over – rain without, sweat within. I called the motel I'd booked and they assured me the shuttle bus would be there in a "jiffy." Now to my understanding that word normally means in no-time-flat. It might have been my imagination, but I waited for close to an hour before my ride appeared. The driver was taciturn to the point of muteness. I wondered if he was angry… ill… rude… deaf… foreign, or what?

The rain still drilled down merrily, but I decided to go in search of milk for the homemade granola my wife had thoughtfully sent along with me. On the way out, I saw in the parking lot a middle-aged couple emerging from what appeared to be a shipping container that occupied one corner of the lot. I can't be sure, but they seemed to be living in there, and visiting the next room to me at the motel. What could be their story?

When I turned in I set the alarm for 3:45 in order to catch the 4:30 shuttle van to the airport. I slept well for about 4 hours, and awoke on my own at 3:50. I checked my alarm. I found that I had uncleverly set it for *PM*. In any case, no problem. No complimentary breakfast, either; they started serving that at five. No matter, I was delivered to SeaTac without incident. I enquired about the driver from the previous evening.

"Oh, Vinnie? Yeah, I sent him home an hour early. Said he had stomach problems."

Eventually, it was time to board the flight. It was the morning of Halloween and several of the passengers and staff were in costume already. Two female airline attendants soberly processed us as we boarded. One was dressed like a witch, and the other – clearly a non-conformist – as a Tootsie Roll. I found the whole thing slightly unsettling. I wondered if the pilot might be gussied up like a skeleton, or perhaps a *9/11 terrorist*.

We landed at Orlando International Airport five hours later. The code for this airport is MCO, and I wondered why. Upon inquiry, I learned that it sits on what was once McCoy Air Force Base. McCoy was operational between 1940 and 1975, and during the Vietnam and Cold Wars was a prominent Strategic Air Command base. I thought of *Dr. Strangelove* and *Fail Safe,* and shivered. Thank God those days are over.

Next morning, after catching up on my sleep and eating a decent breakfast I was ready to roll. It seemed I hadn't had a square meal for days. The breakfast was almost entirely animal-based: pork patties, eggs, cheese, and so on. I usually have little trouble understanding different points of view, but when it comes to *vegetarianism*, I am right out of sympathy. In fact, the prospect of becoming vegetarian fills me with panic – something like giving up, say, *salt.*

Some of the oldest and most vivacious people I have known were dedicated omnivores. According to most studies, many of the supposed health benefits of vegetarianism have been oversold. If I were forced to become a vegetarian, I would fervently hope to be taken quickly to my reward.

Feeling I had the world by the tail, I ordered up a taxi and directed the driver to the Greyhound station downtown. He did a double-take, frowned, shrugged, and we were off. He probably had me pegged for white-trash. I hadn't the slightest idea where we were going, but he seemed to – but the trip went on and on, mile after mile. I was starting to smell a rat, whereupon, suddenly… there we were. The bill was $50, putting a hole in my budget for the day. It must be rare indeed for a taxi driver to get such a princely sum for driving someone to the Greyhound. An unlikely kind of thing, like taking a limo to a thrift store.

The depot was really shocking. It seemed to be full of street-people, disaster-survivors, or refugees. It was an incredible sight, a *defacto* homeless shelter, open to all. There is no chance any of these people was waiting for a bus. I felt pretty conspicuous, but tried to relax and take the scene in. These folks were definitely down-on-their-luck; many wore thick clothes, no doubt for sleeping outdoors.

All ages were there: from babies, to the very old. I not been in such a crush of humanity since spending a glorious evening waiting for the train in New Delhi, immersed in a world of commuters, holy men, mothers, babies, sacred cows, snake charmers, poultry, rats, cats, dogs, bundles of jute, hectic music – all in a delicious miasma of curry and sewage. I loved it all.

Any modern traveler knows that to keep your head above water you need to charge your phone often. Therefore, wherever I go I keep a sharp eye out for an unused electrical outlet – and they can be impossible to find in busy travel centers as everybody's got the same idea. Imagine my surprise, then, when I saw a power bar with an empty spot in it. Plugging into it, however, involved my leaning across a family of about eight, muttering apologies as I went. The spokesman of the group looked me in the eye and said, "Don't worry, brother, it's OK."

I swear, he said that. I felt better, and not so out-of-place, like I was one of the guys, a veritable *brother.*

Being very early for the bus south, I soon unplugged and retired to the depot restaurant – a spartan affair devoid of charm or comfort. However, I met an interesting black man there with whom I fell into conversation. He was perhaps sixty, a retired long-haul trucker. He had twelve children and his wife had died the year before.

I mumbled something sympathetic, at which point he said, "You know, all the same, I do feel blessed." At this point he was speaking so that virtually everyone in the place could hear him. "All I do," he said, "is look to God, and I's just blessed in every way. I even have a honey now I just might marry."

For some reason he had nine hand-crafted walking sticks with him, and he offered me one. Sadly I was unable to accept – I had too much stuff already. He was a lovely and thoughtful man.

After a while, we boarded the bus for points south along Florida Route 1 – Fort Lauderdale, Miami, and so on. Behind me sat a young man and a middle-aged woman, and they were having a wide-ranging, animated discussion on philosophic and theological themes. They were all over the map – a mix, I thought, of good sense and gibberish. They'd just met, and both felt in the mood to talk – and *how* they talked! – in torrents. They even managed to occasionally listen to one another. It wasn't long before I asked to stick my oar in.

The lad had an odd assortment of accomplishments to his name. He was unusually articulate, and noted he'd studied philosophy and psychology in university, similar to myself. I asked him what sort of work he was doing currently. He said in complete earnest, "I'm a fire-breather and sword-swallower in a circus."

To say I was stunned would be a great understatement; I smiled inwardly, and drew closer. "This," I thought, "is going to be interesting."

I'm of the firm opinion that if I'd spent my entire life searching for a fire-breather at random, I'd never have found one. Yet here was one before my very eyes. Such are the experiences and acquaintances to be had for the price of a bus ticket. What could be better?

Naturally I peppered him with questions: how he got into the trade, what are its pros and cons, what's his favorite fuel, who are his mentors, was he going to make a life-career of this sort of thing, and so on. I don't remember everything we talked about, but I do remember him saying that his mother is an acrobat with a circus based in Florida. He and his mother were performing that night in Fort Lauderdale, and he invited me to come along. It pains me that I did not take him up on the offer.

No doubt the children of acrobats seldom take a conventional course in life. As far as I know, I've yet to meet a doctor, lawyer or accountant who had an acrobat anywhere in his lineage. However, this kid was so smart he may end up a physics professor at some hot-shot university.

His theological views struck me as labyrinthine and opaque, but he was confident he had firm command of his material, and clearly loved to expound upon it. There's a lot of that sort of thing on the 'Hound.

His Catholic upbringing had thoroughly put him off Christianity, but still he was fascinated with spiritual things. He spoke in a pedantic way; I recognized elements of Buddhism, Hinduism, New Age and Zoroastrianism. It was like he'd been to a spiritual buffet and stuffed himself to the gills with whatever he fancied. He held what American philosopher-mathematician Martin Gardner termed a 'smorgasbord of fashionable paranormal beliefs.' After listening to him a great while, I shared my own perspective and I hope gave him reason to investigate the Christian faith afresh. In any case, he was most polite, and I liked him very much.

Every so often he pulled out something he called a *Neuralizer* and took a drag on it. It was a weird thing that looked like an electronic syringe. He told me he was trying to quit smoking, and this clever device dispensed nicotine mist that provided a modicum of satisfaction. It was the darnedest thing I ever saw. It struck me odd that a professional fire-breather would care about tobacco smoke one way or the other. I later learned that this was an *electronic cigarette* and they've been available intermittently since 1963. I've no idea why I'd never seen one before; I guess I need to get out more.

Andrew's seat-mate was a woman I'll call 'P,' and she looked worn-out. She lived, she said, in Baltimore, and she was 51. She described herself as an 'advocate and organizer' of the mentally-ill homeless in her area. When I met her she'd been on the bus for 31 hours; she'd been ticking them off precisely as we rolled along. She was feeling, not surprisingly, done-in, grubby and cranky. Nevertheless, she never stopped talking – and there wasn't a single thing she kept secret, including several intriguing gynecologic aspects of her love life. I saw several of her neighbors smile in embarrassment; others guffawed heartily and clamored for more detail.

She'd certainly had had a rough go of it in life: family upheaval, alcoholism, legal trouble, drug abuse, and a recent three-month stretch living under a bridge in Baltimore. It was a dreary litany, indeed. I was not surprised, therefore, when she disclosed she was a client of the Baltimore Mental Health System. She said she was being treated for bipolar illness, PTSD and substance abuse. I have learned that the BMHS has some thirty thousand clients, and venture to say P was likely on their short-list of All Stars.

At one point I heard her call her pharmacy at home. She explained that she'd left Baltimore hurriedly because of a family crisis in Florida, and that she was running out of her prescriptions. She tried to extract a promise from the pharmacist that he would ship her meds to her by the quickest possible means. This piece of business seemed in complete keeping with the chaotic life she had described to all within earshot. Judging by her lack of executive-planning abilities, I would add an additional possible diagnosis, *Adult Attention Deficit Disorder.*

She was vague about her plans, but she was considering moving to Florida to be close to her two grandchildren and daughter – in that order. But naturally there was a problem: her daughter lives with a drug dealer, who can't stand P, and the feeling is mutual. She didn't even know if she'd be welcome to spend that very night under their roof. She said, "I have half a mind to head back to Baltimore."

It's my bet BMHS bought her a one-way ticket.

Early in our three-way conversation she stated categorically Alcoholics Anonymous is a rotten outfit because of all the "God-stuff," and furthermore, "Religion is bunk." She asserted loudly – the whole bus must have heard her – that she was a devout atheist, and *that was that.* You could almost feel her getting her dukes up.

At some point I challenged her about the usefulness of *AA*, which I have seen work wonders, many, many times. But rather than becoming abusive, she was surprisingly respectful, and said she liked to debate these things. Somewhere in the course of the discussion she waxed on about how great illegal drugs are, and how she sort of missed them, especially Quaaludes. She was at pains to make her past life sound so reasonable, so worthy, so cool. It reminded me of one of Dr. Phil McGraw's pet questions, "How's that working for you?"

Just to add interest, she noted that at one stage she'd lived in a polygamous 'intentional community,' which evidently was of great value in her personal development. She hastened to add that, "Everyone was tested."

By the way, I asked her what she thought of Jesus, and she said, "He's cool."

I asked her, if he's so *cool*, why she didn't believe what He taught. This question produced the only spell of silence in the whole afternoon, about thirty seconds. By that time she'd thought of another tangent to be off on, and she was away.

The guy beside me appeared to be rating pretty high on the Glasgow Coma Scale, or he may have been playing possum, technically known as *tonic immobility*. Whatever was going on with him, he was out cold through the animated discussion above.

Just outside Fort Lauderdale we saw a pile-up involving a police car and another vehicle. It was quite a mess, the result of a high-speed chase, by all appearances. I thought in passing, why on earth is it legal to produce vehicles that can easily break every speed law in the world? We have cars with seat belts, air bags, anti-lock brakes, roll bars, crumple zones, five-star accident ratings and all manner of idiot-proofing. Then why, I ask you, allow cars to exceed rational, mandated speed limits – and then send the cops out at break-neck speed to slow them down? This is clearly moronic.

Japan has had a go at this sort of thing. In the mid-seventies, citizens got fed up with carnage on the roads – gangsters in fast cars, highway mayhem and an annual death toll over 10,000. In response, the Japan Automobile Manufacturers Association (JAMA) had a bright idea. This is it: with polite smiles, one imagines, the sages at JAMA suggested limiting the top speed of Japanese cars to 180 km/h. This strict measure, JAMA asserted, would greatly reduce traffic casualties and generally enhance public safety.

It wasn't long till the automotive engineers started complaining that such a restrictive top speed was smothering their creativity. Their creativity consisted in making faster cars and inventing new safety gear to protect drivers from themselves. A certain discontent fermented in the industry. At one point someone suggested doing a *new* study to see if there is *really* a correlation between speed and casualties. The study was conducted. Apparently, common sense plays a tiny role, if any, in the auto business.

In 2004 as a result of the study, JAMA arrived at the astounding conclusion that there is *no* relationship between speed and automobile deaths – which, they added reassuringly, had fallen to a mere 8,000 the previous year. Therefore, they advised abandoning the outdated, snail-like 180km/hr restriction in favor of the more rational and scientific 250. This is rather like saying it won't hurt you any more to jump from the tenth floor of a building than from the second. It's got to be baloney. The investigators were, at best, victims of self-delusion and conflict of interest. I'm all for speed governors on vehicles. The world is far too crowded to allow people to drive around as fast as they like.

We'd finally arrived in Fort Lauderdale, Andrew's home town. It's named after Major William Lauderdale who built a number of forts in the area during the Seminole Wars (1818-1858). The reasons for these wars were unknown to me. I decided to look into the matter.

The Seminoles were an unlikely alliance of three peoples: first were Native Americans of the Creek nation fleeing conflict and colonization in Georgia. Second were the indigenous Apalachee people, and third, runaway slaves called *maroons,* from the South's Low Country. Interestingly, *seminole* means *runaway,* or *wild one.*

By the mid-nineteenth century national policy was such that it was decided to relocate these people to 'Indian Territory' west of the Mississippi. Naturally, the Seminole objected strenuously, and mounted valiant opposition, but to little avail. Virtually all surviving Seminoles were relocated to Oklahoma. It must have been a terribly sad thing for these people.

It's not altogether a tragic tale, however. A remnant group of about 200 Seminoles hid out in the Everglades till things simmered down. The descendants of these courageous folk were eventually accorded federal recognition in 1934 and are in South Florida to this very day. Many Seminoles are involved with the operation of high-stakes bingo casinos, such as the Seminole Classic Casino in Hollywood, near Fort Lauderdale. I do hope they're "sticking it to The Man."

I later found out that the Seminoles are richer than I could have imagined. A bus driver along the way told me that the tribe bought *all* the Hard Rock Cafes in the world in 2007 for eight billion dollars. The company, headquartered in Orlando, owns some 175 restaurants in 53 countries. This tiny ethnic remnant has done rather well for itself, evidently. Only in America!

Andrew said his mother was picking him up at the depot, and she would drive me to my hotel. This did not work out, however; the acrobatic mother didn't show up... I had visions of an aging but svelte woman trying to undo a knot in her left leg. However, he found me the most charming black cabbie, and saw me on my way, with profuse best wishes flying in all directions.

I was in a taxi of the Yellow line with the fantastic phone number 777-7777. I started to wonder – why are there so many Yellow cabs wherever you go? Are they related in some way, or is it just a convenient convention to have cabs liveried in this conspicuous color? Well, it turns out that there are bright yellow taxis the world over, and most are not related corporately to one another.

The Yellow Taxicab Company was incorporated in New York City in 1912; it charged the unimaginable sum of fifty cents a mile. Two years later a company calling itself the Yellow Cab Company started operating in Chicago. A study conducted at the august University of

Chicago concluded that *yellow* was the easiest car color to spot; I'm serious. You wouldn't think they'd need a special study to come to that conclusion – just ask anybody.

There are variants of the Yellow Cab Company all over North America and Australia; the biggest one is in Chicago. Most of the taxis in India have bright yellow roofs, and can be seen a mile away. The cabbie and I – I wish I'd learned his name – talked mostly of the upcoming presidential election. He was a very jolly fellow, a Pentecostal who had "no – and I do mean *no* – use for Mr. Romney," and thought that he was a "terrible liar."

He was naturally a big Obama fan, but he worried corruption in high places might spoil his chances for re-election in Florida. I only got half what he was saying, but he was so good-humored and sensible I fell over myself to give him a nice tip.

What a day it was… my idea of a good time.

That evening I went for a ramble through the northern part of Fort Lauderdale. It was flat, like the whole state, and featureless, but it felt good to be using my legs. After seeking diversion in this manner for some miles, I spied a restaurant with the catchy name of *Chicken Kitchen*. I was the only customer; I bought a Deluxe Pollo Suprimo Wrap, a fabulous thing with myriad ingredients, and an icy glass bottle of lovely purple grape juice. The wrap was extremely good; the lady who served me had a rather maternal attitude; I think she wanted to make sure I was eating properly.

My hotel was a big, impersonal, overrated place… but I slept well. My cabbie the next morning was marvelous. Twenty years ago he was one of a band of Haitians that made it to Florida over hundreds of miles of open ocean in a dilapidated boat. They just showed up here, and behold: he is now an American citizen, the driver of a smart Fort Lauderdale Yellow Cab, a proud husband and the father of three children, the older two of whom are doing well in a local college. This fellow's life is a real wonder, and he gives thanks accordingly. He said that the relatives of Haitian dictator Papa Doc Duvalier thought they were *gods*, but he declared, "You gotta realize, my fren,' only Gawd is Gawd!" Just so.

He told me he plans to retire in Haiti – which is, "Heaven on Earth if'n you got money." He thought his children might try to thwart this idea. All told, he was a perfect gent and a godly man; he gave me a bunch of tracts to distribute. If anyone said to me that miracles don't happen any more, I would point to this lovely and blessed man.

I just love friendly, thoughtful cabbies.

At the Greyhound station I dealt with an agent whose tag said *Ashley*. She politely looked after the formalities. Then I noticed her fingernails, no doubt the pride of her young life. They were so long – two full inches – that I wondered how on earth she was able to get any work done. I wish I'd photographed them. They were perfectly enameled, umpteen coats no doubt, and a unique color scheme, all spots and slashes, something like a kaleidoscope.

I said, "Those are the greatest nails I ever saw." Being perhaps unacquainted with my brand of irony, she beamed with pleasure. I beamed back.

Nor was that all that was remarkable about Miss Ashley. She had the most remarkable upper eyelashes I've ever seen. They looked like two fuzzy little birds – crow hatchlings, I'd say, perched right up there. I decided to keep any more comments to myself, or she might put me on the wrong bus. I kind of wished her name were more fitting – Tryxella, maybe.

The reason I travel is mostly insatiable curiosity. I don't visit places to indulge in the conventional pleasures, but rather more as an investigative reporter might visit a crime scene, or an astronaut might enjoy visiting a new planet, or a deep-sea diver might try to find out what happens on the sea-bed. Travel is hardwired within me, it surely is.

In a sense, I feel like a secret agent who's been dropped behind enemy lines to gather intelligence. Every day on the road is different

– literally *unique*. Most days are interesting one way or another, some are weird, some wondrous, some disturbing. In my experience there are very few days on the road that you'd call duds. Even a miserable day can provide fodder for an amusing memory.

The bus ride today was a quiet affair; mostly I just read. From Miami south, there was hardly anyone aboard. I tried striking up some talk with the only other passenger, a strange man of about 60 years, and to all appearances, they'd been hard ones. He was about 300 pounds, with a brown-grey ponytail down to his waist, a beard that went in all directions, and an orange woolen toque with matching suspenders. I'd love to have asked him what on earth he was wearing the toque for, but likely he'd have thought I was way too nosy for my own good. I heard him say to the driver, whom I think he knew, that there was a pretty lady waiting for him at the bar in Duck Key.

I'd loved to have been a fly on the wall in that bar when they met that evening. Says he, "Hi Honey… yore shore lookin' mi-dee purdy this evenin.'"

She smiles, bats her lashes, and replies, "Hey big boy, yer not so bad yerself. Lookin' for some trouble, are ya?"

I was trying to picture what might happen next, when I suddenly realized where we were; we were entering Key Largo. I snapped out of my reverie.

The first I'd heard of Key Largo was in the 1948 Bogart *film noir* of the same name directed by John Huston. It's a great yarn about gangsters, guns, molls, lawmen, Seminoles, an approaching hurricane and serious chemistry between Bogart and Bacall – all in glorious black and white. I was disappointed to learn that apart from background filming used for establishing shots, the filming was done entirely on a Warner Brothers sound stage in Hollywood. It's still a marvelous and atmospheric film. Edward G. Robinson as Cuban hoodlum Johnny Rocco was simply perfect.

At the north end of Key Largo was a billboard that caught my eye.

It was advertising a famous line of fishing lures called Rapala, from Finland. There was a picture of a game fish – a tarpon, I think – eying a flashy lure. It said, quite simply, *Seafood's Seafood*. I had to read it a couple of times to get it; I thought it was terrific, and the ad has obviously stuck with me. I actually use Rapala lures at home.

After the charmer in the orange toque got off the bus looking for love in Duck Key, there was only one other passenger, a garrulous Latino, a lively chap who turned out to be a marine mechanic from Key West. I changed seats to be able to talk to him and the driver. He kept phoning his wife to keep her posted on his progress.

At one point, he said to me, "You know about iguanas?"

I admitted my abysmal ignorance of the subject; he seemed eager to contribute to my education. He pointed out a few of them sitting on the right side of the road, at right angles to it, facing east, like sun-worshipers at dawn. He said they are not native to the Keys, but are thought to be the progeny of an escaped pregnant female pet iguana. Or, he added, maybe it was a couple of pet iguanas that eloped; who can say? They have no natural enemies, he said, because their skin secretes a deadly poison. He said, however, when *skinned* they make marvelous eating, largely because they subsist on a vegetarian diet. I had visions of a giant hot dog with a skinned, nicely broiled iguana tail inside, complete with spicy mustard, a side of onion rings, and a cold draft beer. I resolved to look around Key West for a place that dishes up that sort of thing.

I asked about the fresh water supply here and was astonished to learn that it's all sent down by pipeline by the Florida Keys Aqueduct Authority. This supplier taps into the south Florida aquifer in an environmentally-protected rocky pine forest west of Florida City, near the Everglades. I recalled seeing the aqueduct on my way through the Keys; it's suspended above the ocean, about 100 yards to the east of the Overseas Highway. The water is naturally hard and is treated to make it softer; a disinfectant is also added. The pipeline is 130 miles long and has a diameter starting at 36 inches, tapering at the Key West end to 18 inches. Enormous electric pumps send the water southward, augmented by booster pumps along the way. In case of emergencies, the system can be run with diesel pumps; desalination plants are standing by. Fresh water is taken seriously here.

Peering at the passing scene, something put me in mind of the penal colony on Devil's Island in French Guiana. The mangrove swamps looked unsympathetic, and I imagined the murky backwaters must be full of malign creatures – sharks, jellyfish, barracudas, alligators, electric eels – God knows what. With some effort I shook off the pessimism; never mind… I was here, and I was going to make the best of it.

By late afternoon, we rolled into Key West, right onto South Roosevelt Drive. The driver announced our arrival on the PA system. The fact that the bus was empty apart from him and me didn't get in the way of normal procedure. As I got off the bus, I thanked him sincerely for his pleasantness and competence. There's absolutely nothing like a fella who's happy at his work. Bus drivers fall into two groups, the one's who like the job, and the others that hate the job – mainly because they despise the clientele.

Key West is a compact little city; the bus driver said, "Why, it's only but five miles around." The local population of 25,000 was about the same a century ago. The locals are known as *conchs*, pronounced 'konks.' The local understanding is that conchs are of two classes: *saltwater conchs*, who were born in Key West, and *freshwater conchs* who have lived there for at least seven years. The local motto is *One Human Family*. From what I'd heard, *Anything Goes* would be more like it.

Many of the original settlers were from the Bahamas. They arrived in the early years of the American Revolution, and their descendants live in a part of town known as *Bahama Village*. The other main group of settlers were, of course, Cubans. Their main pursuit seems to have been the production of cigars. At one point in the 19th century there were fully *two hundred* cigar factories in town, producing an astounding *100 million* cigars a year. Can you imagine? If all those cigars were laid end to end (allowing six inches per cigar), they would literally cover the distance from Key West to Calcutta. They must have produced enough smoke to fill all of creation. It's a wonder the world survived.

By the mid-1800s the average Key West resident was the richest in the nation, mainly from the avails of salvaging ships, an activity known as *wrecking*. One historian notes with a wink that the place was known for its 'unusually high concentration of fine furniture and chandeliers.' I thought of the novel, *Jamaica Inn,* by Daphne Du Maurier, set in Cornwall. In it appears the old Cornish prayer:

O Lord, we pray Thee, not that wrecks should happen, but if they do happen,

Thou wilt guide them to the coast of Cornwall for the benefit of the poor inhabitants.

I can imagine early Key West wreckers setting aside their cigars for a moment, and praying in like manner. Whether they prayed or not, they did very well for themselves.

I found another point of local history interesting. Pan American Airlines was founded in Key West in 1927, and many years later became the biggest airline in the country. Pan Am started as a mail and passenger service between Key West and Havana. The aircraft they used in the early days was the Sikorsky S-43, a 'flying boat' known as the *Baby Clipper*.

I'd love to have taken one of their early, deafening flights to Havana – what excitement… what romance! I'd likely have run into Ernest Hemingway; we might have gone fishing together and had some fun. What would Havana have been like in those heady days? Bursting with color, clamor, music, intrigue… all in a gorgeous, blue bank of cigar-smoke.

The later history of Pan Am was indeed tragic. The airline was iconic, a symbol of what some saw as overweening American pride;

its prominence attracted the attention of iconoclasts on a mission to humiliate the country. On December 21,1988 a terrorist bomb destroyed Pan Am Flight 103 over Lockerbie, Scotland, with the loss of 270 lives. The resulting lawsuits crippled Pan Am. Its financial situation was worsened by the Persian Gulf War of 1990-91, when high fuel prices discouraged air travel. The once-glorious Pan Am went bankrupt in 1991.

It was only a mile to my hotel, so I decided to hoof it, rolling my little bag behind me. I took a few deep breaths, filling my lungs with delicious salty, sunny air. The feeling of freedom and anticipation was tremendous. I walked along South Roosevelt Boulevard, right along the water – brilliant sunshine, lovely breeze in my face, pelicans and terns overhead. I saw a bunch of locals tossing nets off the seawall, and stopped to see what they were catching. They told be they were netting bait-fish; it was a lovely scene, and these fellows were glad to instruct me in their art.

I feel I've arrived somewhere interesting when I see pelicans in flight. I really like them –for their combination of ugliness, power and competence. Like everything in nature, their design is perfect for the life they lead. There are many kinds and colors of pelican, but the *brown* ones favor this area. Pelicans have an enormous distribution: as far south as Tasmania and as far north as western Canada. In terms of altitude they can be found from below sea-level – all the way to 10,000 feet. It is said a mother pelican will tear her own breast to feed her young when other food is unavailable. This is one versatile bird.

There are several mystical attributes attached to the pelican. In ancient Egypt it was believed to facilitate transition to the underworld. St. Thomas Aquinas wrote a hymn called *Humbly We Adore Thee*. In it he describes Christ as the loving divine pelican, able to provide nourishment from His breast. And, as if to emphasize the spiritual significance of this multifaceted fowl, a pelican feeding her young was

depicted at the bottom of the title page of the first edition of the King
James Bible in 1611.

Such is the historical and mystical significance of the pelican that
both Oxford and Cambridge Universities have colleges named Corpus
Christi whose respective crests depict the pelican pecking its breast
to feed its young. And finally, at the risk of inducing pelican *ennui*,
I discovered that Sir Francis Drake's famous ship the *Golden Hind*
was originally named *Pelican*. The image of this ship appeared on the
English Halfpenny for many years.

I saw a truly shocking event when on the beach in Mexico a few
years ago. A portly, pallid, bald tourist was disporting himself in waist-
deep water a few yards from shore. Just then a pelican, likely 30 pounds
of him, spotted a fish close by, and dived at full speed. Unfortunately
for the wader, the bird's huge bill dealt him a savage gash on his head.
The man collapsed... bloody billows filled the water, people rushed
to help. The man was nearly killed. Not likely this fellow went home
with any fond or mystical sentiments about pelicans.

The next morning, I awoke and remembered that we had just re-
verted to standard time. Because I am a lover of the light, this day in
November is normally tinged with dread for me – the dying of the
light, the coming of the dark chill. However, on this day, with the sun
shining in a cloudless sky, grumbling was the last thing on my mind.

I decided to take a ramble around town on foot. The man who
booked me in the night before suggested that I should use the hotel's
free shuttle bus to go downtown. I said that I was a keen walker; he
looked at me dubiously, and his young Slavic assistant warned that
there was a lot of construction to be navigated. He hinted darkly that
there were hazards to be encountered when walking around town; he
wouldn't do it if he were me. Well, he wasn't me, and such advice
brings out my inner contrarian.

I set off that morning seeking breakfast, for one thing, and I also
wanted to see if I could check out a B&B called The Angelina, a place

of excellent repute, located on Angela Street. I found the Burger King in an unpromising neighborhood in the middle of a sewer construction zone, on North Roosevelt Drive. The little fellow behind the counter unsmilingly awaited my order, entirely dead-pan. The next instant, he was in an animated shouting-match with a co-worker in back. They were shouting in Haitian Creole. I have no idea what they were shouting about, but they really went at it.

The staff took its sweet time assembling my breakfast, while I stood there whistling and looking at the ceiling. As I waited, a tall black gent came in and asked if it was "too early to get a Whopper." The lad on the counter said it was indeed too early, and advised the potential diner to return in ten minutes. I observed the body language between the two. There was not a trace of warmth or expression on either side. I stayed in the place for another half-hour, and he never came back.

There was only one other customer in the place – a fellow with a grimy backpack pack, a greasy hat and thick glasses. He sat behind me. With three big books on the table in front of him, he was applying himself to what looked like a hardcover novel from the library. I didn't know what to make of him exactly, but I imagine he was a gentle, literate homeless soul, a bibliophile with nowhere to go except to Burger King and the public library.

Looking back on the breakfast experience, I found myself thinking of the significance of the human smile. When one is traveling in a far country, smiles to me are like a cup of water to a thirsty man; as Proverbs has it, *a cheerful look brings joy to the heart.*

I've noticed Americans smile a great deal more than most other nationalities – especially the politicians; Vice-President Joe Biden is an extreme example – *acres* of enamel. Smiles often lack sincerity, of course, but they *are* part of everyday courtesy in this country, and when a smile is not forthcoming, I miss it. Among humans, smiling expresses pleasure, often friendliness, happiness, or amusement. I've heard it takes fewer facial muscles to smile than to frown, and that smiling gives you a shot of endorphins. I'm all for smiling.

The significance of the smile varies across cultures. The Thai people are said to have fourteen kinds of smile, one even for when there's no reason to smile. If you smile at a stranger in Russia, you're liable to be thought a suspicious character. This notion may be a hold-over from the old Soviet regime; Stalin looked terrifying when he smiled. Come to think of it, I never saw a smile on any of those dreary old *Politburo* gangsters. With Vladimir Putin a smile is unusual, ephemeral and chilling.

The subject of the smile came home to me that morning when I was trying to conduct some routine business with the front desk of the hotel. I smiled at the young woman who stepped up to help me. She did not smile back, which unsettled me a bit. When she started to speak I realized she was of Slavic background. I asked her an innocent question, something like, "How do you get to city hall?"

She didn't reply; her face expressed absolutely nothing – just blank. I wondered if she understood me and asked her so.

She then assumed a haughty, wounded tone although her face remained as plain as a bowl of porridge, and said, "Vell, I do spik Engleesh!"

I said I hoped I hadn't offended her – vain hope! She said I had not, with the same catatonic expression as before. It was an odd experience in my books, and quite dashed my spirits. I was pretty lonesome to start with, and this girl's attitude was salt in my wound.

To return to my narrative, I walked for miles through this compact city, through overgrown and slightly dilapidated neighborhoods that were quiet and rather charming. No one seemed to be about. I passed the huge Key West City Cemetery located on Passover Lane in the middle of town. Within were hundreds of above-ground graves dating from the 1840s. There are a number of cultural influences represented there, mainly African, Anglo and Hispanic. Even at mid-day the place felt unsettling to me; I felt as if I spent much time there, I might be swept into a vortex involving the terrors of the departed.

I'm no expert in cemeteries, but of the ones I've visited, the quality of humor is demonstrably lacking. Not so this one. In the local tourist guide, its location is given as the 'dead center of town.' Upon some of the gravestones are riotous inscriptions such as *I told you I was sick*, and *At least I know where he's sleeping tonight.* The gravestone of one General Abraham Lincoln Sawyer notes that he was forty inches tall, and always wanted a 'man-sized grave.' One imagines a pint-sized Uncle Sam, wrapped in the *Stars and Stripes* lying beneath the sod. What can you say? This is Key West.

I located the Angelina after a fairly complex bit of navigating the choppy streets of Old Key West. It had a *No Vacancy* sign outside, but I went in anyway. I asked the lady at the desk if the paucity of vacancies was permanent, or if there might be an opening in the foreseeable future. She furrowed her brow and commented on "how busy" she'd been. She did find one night free the following week, but I told her that sadly it wouldn't do for me. She smiled and shrugged; we parted amicably. She had a wonderful smile, and surely knew how to treat prospective guests, even an apparent no-account walk-in.

As I walked the streets, a rather dissipated fellow of about fifty went by operating a pedi-cab, a sort of tricycle rickshaw. He and I were the only two people on the block. The passenger seats were empty, and yet he did not make eye contact with me, nor did he ask if perchance I fancied a ride. In keeping with this man's general lassitude, I noticed an ad on the back of his conveyance. It was for Captain Morgan Rum. Alongside a dashing depiction of the captain himself were these words:

> *Here's to great days and better nights.*
> *Here's to Life, Love and Loot!*

You see pictures of the mephistophelian captain all over town. Honestly, there are so many pictures and effigies of Captain Henry Morgan around Key West, you'd think he was running for mayor. The actual Henry Morgan (1635–1688) was a Welsh privateer and pirate who plundered the 'Spanish Main,' an area covering Florida, the Gulf of Mexico, the Caribbean and the north coast of South America. His first name was actually *Harri*, which to me sounds awfully tame for a pirate. Perhaps with a name like that he was afraid people would think him a pantywaist, so he became a pirate. By all accounts he really was a ruthless scoundrel, but a skillful one – ranking ninth in *Forbes* list of top-earning pirates. The editors of *Forbes* must have time on their hands.

Dear Harri ended his sojourn on Earth, as many career criminals do, as a respected member of society – in his case, Jamaican. In the end, he was a knight, an admiral of the Royal Navy, and Lieutenant Governor of Jamaica. He died at 55, of tuberculosis and, some say, "drink." He was interred at Palisadoes cemetery, which slumped into the sea in the earthquake in 1692. Appropriate, don't you think?

Some poster boy.

The rum that takes its name from this charmer is produced in Puerto Rico by Diageo, plc, of London, the world's largest producers of alcoholic beverages. Diageo blesses the world with 70,000,000 liters of Captain Morgan annually; it is the second most-consumed liquor in the U.S. Apparently, the Captain is still up to his tricks.

Later, I took a stroll down Duval Street – named for William Pope Duval (1784–1854), first governor of Florida, a thoroughly decent chap by all accounts. It is the main tourist drag and, I regret to say, a thoroughly dreary parade of bars, strip clubs, and clip-joints. I was interested to find it had been accorded 'Great Street' status by the American Planning Association in 2012. What on earth were they thinking? More like "Greatly-Disappointing Street" in my books.

The whole place was pervaded by a listlessness, a malaise, brought on, I believe, by incessant efforts to excite the lust of surging hordes of out-of-towners. I passed one bar and looked in. Lengthwise on the bar lay a young woman in the briefest garb with a full shot-glass on her navel. A customer was trying to pick up the glass and drink its contents using only his mouth. The scene made me sad; who was this girl? Who were her parents?

When I got part-way down the street, I got the distinct feeling that exhaustion had set in among these purveyors of eroticism. The street put me in mind of an impotent man trying to cure himself by watching porn all day. Duval Street, indeed, seemed like an old hooker in the form of a street. It was boring as Hell.

I passed one door over which was a sign which read *Gentleman's Entertainment Club.* I heard music thumping inside the place; it was Bob Seger's *Night Moves:*

> *...workin' on mysteries without any clues,*
> *workin' on our night moves...*

A young woman with tousled red hair stuck her head out and beckoned, "Hey, mister... c'meer!" She reminded me of the Greek sirens of whom has been written, *Their song, though irresistibly sweet, was no less sad than sweet, lapped both body and soul in a fatal lethargy, the forerunner of death and corruption.*

In *The Odyssey,* the hero lashed himself to the mast of his ship to avoid yielding to the sirens' call. This seemed a sound strategy to me, but having no mast handy, I made my escape by hot-footing it out of there. Then and there I decided I'd had enough sleaze for the time being.

Down the street was another establishment, with the soul-numbing name The Dungeon of Dark Secrets and Fetishes. There was a sign urging me to attend *Drag Shows Nightly,* and to be sure not to miss the *Dance to the Sun-God T Dance,* "coming soon." Sorry, folks, not my cup of tea.

Nearby was a billboard trumpeting the good life in Key West. It was captioned, *Your fly's down and you couldn't be happier.* More like *Kink West,* if you ask me.

What would you look like after a few days of sampling the delights of Duval Street? The prospect makes the mind reel. Many of the locals looked as though they might say something like, "I came here for a week's vacation twenty years ago, and just never left." It puts me in mind of the famous line in *Hotel California:*

> *You can check-out any time you like, but you can never leave.*

Duval Street was, for me, perfectly ironical, bearing in mind Key West bills itself as *Paradise*. My dictionary defines *paradise* as the abode of righteous souls after death; an intermediate resting place for righteous souls awaiting the Resurrection; a place of ideal loveliness; and a state of delight. Key West? I think not.

The unswerving pursuit of decadence achieves a certain crescendo on Duval Street: a paroxysm of decay – a carious tooth in the long mandible of Florida. In another Eagles song is the line,

> *Call some place paradise, and kiss it good-bye.*

At one point, a hefty middle-aged babe in pink on a Harley zipped by; she wore no helmet and talked gaily on a cell phone in her left hand. I hesitate to use any word connected with gay, gaiety, and the like, especially in this locale, where it is reported that two in five of the local population are of that persuasion. The word *gay,* incidentally, is of Germanic origin, meaning *quick* or *sudden*. Modern dictionaries are in quite a ferment as to how to define the word.

To illustrate local attitudes, I cite the Nov. 2, 2012 edition of *KEY WEST THE NEWSPAPER*. This publication is also known as the *Blue Paper;* its motto is *Journalism as a Contact Sport*. The lead story concerned Omar Barrera, 22, described as a local 'pretty boy.' On the night of May 28, Chief of Police Donnie Lee entertained Omar at his home. Evidently the Chief's hospitality was not up to scratch in Omar's view, and he started yelling abuse at the Chief who, reasonably enough, showed the boy the door. In fact the Chief escorted him to his car, a '98 Mustang. The lad was thoroughly intoxicated, but the Chief helped him get rolling anyway. He got rolling, all right… backwards. He ran smack into the chain-link fence of the neighboring Quality Inn. One can imagine the pandemonium at the QI: Lights switched on… people wandering out on their balconies in their PJs, demanding to know what the devil was going on.

The article listed the reparations, and made particular note that the fence repair totaled $1,225. Significantly, any thought of charging the *chief* with anything never actually arose. A few local spoil-sports suggested the Chief be disciplined for helping a drunk drive off, but that came to nothing. Not a word was written about any possible un-seemliness concerning the Chief of Police hosting an overnighter for a 'pretty boy.' This *is* Key West, after all.

I happened upon the Key West AIDS Memorial, at the south end of White Street, on the ocean at the southernmost point of the country. It's a large granite area laid into the sidewalk. A sign noted Key West has lost more than a thousand of its residents to AIDS. The privately-funded memorial was dedicated on World AIDS Day in 1997, at which time it held the names of 730 individuals. There is space for 1,500 names; each year more are added. A group called Friends of the Key West AIDS Memorial takes care of it.

You won't get far in Key West before you encounter the name Jimmy Buffet. I think they have his music coming from hidden speakers all over town. I actually like a lot of his tunes – cleverly-worded, relaxed, funny, easy to hum. A favorite of mine is *Cheeseburger in Paradise*; here are a few lines:

> *Tried to amend my carnivorous habits*
> *Made it nearly seventy days*
> *Losin' weight without speed, eatin' sunflower seeds*
> *Drinkin' lots of carrot juice and soakin' up rays*
> *But at night I'd had these wonderful dreams*
> *Some kind of sensuous treat*
> *Not zucchini, fettucini or Bulgar wheat*
> *But a big warm bun and a huge hunk of meat....*

It's a kind of music some call 'island escapism'; his fans rather unflatteringly call themselves *Parrotheads*. I took it upon myself to acquaint myself with his career.

The good Mr. Buffet was born on Christmas day in 1946. As well as being a singer-songwriter and founder of the slyly-named *Coral Reefer Band*, he is a best-selling author and businessman, having controlling interest in two restaurant chains – the Cheeseburger in Paradise line, with 34 locations nationwide, and the Margaritaville Cafe group, one of which is located at 500 Duval Street. Speaking of escapism, in my haste to escape Duval Street, I missed the Buffet place altogether.

Key West's other famous resident is Ernest Hemingway. He's a writer whose work, I'm sad to say, never much appealed to me – my shortcoming, no doubt. Even the slimmest of his books, *The Old Man and the Sea* I had to strain to finish. I had a go at several others, but I found his style just a bit too *spare* and *tight,* as his commentators call it. I do however recall a couple of statements he made about writing that ring true. One of his admirers, a would-be writer, gushed that she would *love* to be a writer if only she could find the time. He thought for a moment, then said something like, "So what do you do between two and five in the morning?" That is a wonderful line, and a fine goad. The other thing I remember is that he called any first draft – "rubbish."

In any case, Hemingway lived in Key West intermittently in the thirties; while there he worked on *Death in the Afternoon*, *For Whom the Bell Tolls* and *The Snows of Kilimanjaro*. Interestingly, his only novel set in America is *To Have and Have Not*, published in 1937. It was set in Depression-era Key West, and was later made into a movie in 1944, starring Bogie and Bacall. I saw it recently, and it is stylish and a pleasure to watch, but the content is mighty thin. To director Howard Hawks, Hemingway himself said it was his worst book, and "full of junk."

His favorite bar was Sloppy Joe's at 201 Duval Street; it's still there, and upon casual inspection, as sloppy as ever. To judge from the street, its upkeep hasn't cost the owners more than a couple of bucks since it was founded in 1933. The original Sloppy Joe's is in Havana; named after owner Jose Garcia Rio who, it is said, ran a sloppy outfit indeed, full of smugglers and deadbeats. Hemingway suggested the name for the Key West branch. Since 1981, it has been the site of the annual Ernest Hemingway look-alike contest.

Hemingway's passions were legendary, larger than life, as they say. Hardware store owner Charles Thompson introduced Hemingway to big-game fishing; he was hooked immediately. *Papa* was wild about many things – hunting, boxing, bullfighting, boozing, brawling – all *macho* stuff. He must also have had an optimistic interest in getting married, which he did four times.

An odd fact about Hemingway is that he had a cat named 'Snowball' that had seven toes on each foot. Snowball's descendants still roam the grounds of his old house on Whitehead Street. No one is sure how many cats there are, but informed opinion suggests *dozens*. These cats must have received special dispensation from City Council who have ruled that the maximum number of animals per household is *four*. Judging by what I saw in Key West, this may be its sole by-law.

Hemingway's last days were really terrible. In 1960 he began a rather rapid physical and mental decline. He was wracked with anxiety, paranoia and depression, exacerbated by his heavy drinking. Seeking peace and quiet, his wife Mary took him to Ketchum, in the mountains of Idaho. Papa's decline continued. In December he was admitted to the Mayo Clinic in Minnesota under a false name where he was treated aggressively with electro-convulsive therapy (ECT). Nothing worked; he spent days on end in bed. Finally, on July 2, 1961 he took his own life with his 'favorite' shotgun, as commentators have grimly noted. The press was told that the death was accidental, and he was accorded a dignified Catholic funeral. It was fully five years later that Mary admitted her husband had committed suicide.

Before we leave Hemingway in peace, there's one more thing. A few years ago I saw a memorable film called *Wrestling Ernest*

Hemingway with Robert Duvall, Richard Harris, Shirley MacLaine and Sandra Bullock. The Harris character, full of fantastic boasts, claimed to have wrestled Hemingway to a draw. It's a story set in Miami about the search for love and meaning in old age. As a study in loneliness in the elderly, I think it's matchless. I really liked it, but it was so close to home, I could hardly endure it.

On my second day in Key West, I decided to rent a bicycle, mainly because my poor flat feet ached like fury. This rig was a real bargain: $15 for a full day, complete with map, lock, helmet and flashing red light. The rental contract suggested helpfully that the light was for 'use after dark.'

And what a marvel this old bike was – a lovely yellow, slightly battered, utterly retro Schwinn Coaster – no gears, no hand controls, big basket, just the kind of bike everyone rode when I was about seven. The brake was fine, but it took some practice for me to stop as though I knew what I was doing. I tossed a few victuals into my backpack and set out in the direction of the bus depot, intent upon circumnavigating the city, which I reckoned was five miles of level peddling.

I traveled along till I reached the Overseas Highway, heading north. There wasn't much traffic, so I decided to go in that direction, which involves leaving Key West itself by way of a short bridge that deposited me on Stock Island. On this island, of which I had never heard, are located a surprising number of interesting things. These caught eye: the Florida Keys Memorial Hospital, Florida Keys Community College, Monroe County Detention Center and the 18-hole Key West Golf Club, sitting proudly on 200 acres.

The first place I encountered, however, was the Key West Tropical Forest and Botanical Garden. I wheeled in and locked my bike to a palm tree. No one was anywhere to be seen, so I ambled toward the main gate. At one point, a sign directed me to the right, if I wanted to see the *Cuban Chugs* display. Not sure what I was getting into, I marched in that direction. What I saw there was really one of the most remarkable sights of my life.

It was a collection of watercraft called *chugs,* used by various groups of Cubans that have made their way to Florida on their own, and entirely without permission. I looked closer. Some of these craft were recognizable as boats, but some were more like rafts, while others looked a total jumble, one notch above flotsam. All were inventively designed and built – outlandish, really – and by virtue of their being in Florida at all, rather miraculously up to the job.

The one I liked the best was a steel craft, a respectable open boat, painted sky blue. It had lovely lines, and an American flag drawn on either side of the sleek bow. Perhaps to save space and paint, there were but fourteen stars and six stripes, but the sight was truly moving. You could picture the painter, intent upon a better life, drawing with great care, even love, this homage to his dream. Perhaps the most amazing feature of this boat, which was about twenty feet long, was that it was made of oil drums. These drums were split open, then flattened, shaped and riveted together. Pretty smart! I'll bet the builder is a prosperous American citizen by now, perhaps a builder of yachts. I'd love to know.

Another of the chugs made me doubt my own eyes. It was a disorderly agglomeration of what seemed random material. First of all, I simply could not believe this pile of stuff had been able to bring its human cargo across the perilous Straits of Florida – an expanse of ninety-three miles known for contrary currents, sharks and Coast Guard patrols. It had a frame of steel bars, those used for reinforcing concrete. The bars were wired together. Over this was laid blue tarpaulin material, wired to the frame. The interior of this creation was half-filled with sea-sponges – for comfort, one imagines, as well as flotation. Come to think of it, its main advantage was the fact that it simply could not sink. It likely sat so low in the water it could evade detection by sight or radar. My bet is that the Coast Guards of both countries are silently cheering for these boat-people, and make only enough arrests to protect their own jobs. Who wouldn't sympathize with these courageous and ingenious people?

I did eventually arrive at the main gate; I saw a woman of about seventy sitting at a desk, looking at a picture-book. She greeted me very politely, even warmly. After a few courtesies, she pointed out that the park was closing shortly, but if I wanted to pay for admission right then, she'd write a note on my ticket granting me admission the next day. I went for it, mainly to legitimize my taking her time, because I intended to grill her about the Cubans and their chugs.

Her name was Josefina, and a gracious lady she was. She told me she had been born in Cuba and come to the U.S. at the age of seven. I immediately wondered if she'd come in one of the chugs that had so captured by imagination. No, she said, she had come by plane. Her family had left Cuba just before *La Revolucion,* which began in 1953. I asked if refugees are still arriving these days. She said indeed they are – in fact a boat carrying fifteen landed on the beach near her house just the month before. She told me that if these Cubans manage to touch American soil – or sand, or coral, I guess – they can legally stay, and pursue citizenship. However, if they do get interdicted by the American authorities, they get speedily repatriated. I'd like to know how many attempts it usually takes to succeed.

In 1980 the Cuban economy tanked, producing an enormous increase in the number of people prepared to try their luck getting to America. Initially appearing to resist this trend, President Fidel Castro finally announced that anyone who wanted to leave by boat could do so. An enormous exodus known as the *Mariel Boatlift* resulted. Key West was soon awash in refugees; close to 125,000 Cubans entered the U.S. this way between the Spring and Fall of that year. Subsequently these events became rather a vexation to American authorities, when it was learned the 'refugees' were, in fact, largely the result of 'cleaning out' Cuba's prisons and mental facilities. Fidel the fox.

Incredibly, this influx of Cubans led to the short-lived 'secession' of the City of Key West from the rest of the country, in April 1982. The U.S. Border Patrol had become concerned with the number of Cubans of dubious background attempting to reach the Florida mainland. I'm not sure why that was such an issue – they were on U.S. soil anyway – but in any case, a blockade of the northbound lanes of the Overseas Highway was set up at Florida City. Every northbound vehicle was stopped and its occupants interrogated. This resulted in a monumental impediment to normal commerce; the Keys were paralysed; the queue of cars trying to leave the Keys stretched seventeen miles at one stage. Tourists stayed away in droves.

The *secessionistas* dubbed their 'new country' *The Conch Republic.* In celebration, assorted memorabilia were produced – flags, T-shirts, mugs, hats and so on; I'm told these things still sell at a good clip. This declaration was symbolic, and mainly tongue-in-cheek, I gather, although there were likely some sincere local firebrands. Note that the Conch Republic Independence Celebration occurs annually on April 23. The motto of the movement was *we seceded where others failed.* This is technically untrue, of course, but it *is* a snappy and amusing saying, eminently worthy of Margaritaville.

By Wednesday, November 6, I'd had my fill of Key West. I was getting lonesome, and I figured it was about time to head for home. When I prepared to check out I was afraid I'd have to deal with the woman who bruised my ego two days before. Sure enough, at seven in the morning, there she was, behind the counter. "Ah, so, Mr. Vat-son, you are leaving us?" She was so utterly pleasant I could scarcely believe it. Maybe there were twin sisters working there, and this was the nice one. Maybe there was only one, and she was happy I was going.

A moment before I'd been ready to let her have it if she gave me any lip, but instead I became a trifle mesmerized by her eyes and smile. I'm going to say she was Hungarian, and it doesn't bother me a bit if she can't pronounce the letter *W* like I do; maybe she even does it the right way, for all I know. Besides, I rather like the sound of "Vat-son"

– sounds rather Eastern European cloak-and-dagger to me. If I didn't clear out of there smartly, I figured, I might become putty in her hands. In twenty years I'd have become a burnt-out homeless octogenarian freshwater conch hanging out at Sloppy Joe's. It was that close.

I began to walk to the bus depot, which is located at Key West International Airport. This place is a veritable *transport hub*. A taxi with the unforgettable name MAXI TAXI sped by. When I arrived, the Greyhound agent, a very pleasant grey-haired man, inspected my passport. He asked me where in Canada I was from, and seemed genuinely interested. He said that he had a 'bucket list' with included a long tour to the Yukon and Alaska – by Greyhound, of course! He was particularly keen to see Dawson City. I encouraged him, suggesting he familiarize himself with the work of Robert Service and Jack London. You have no business going there if you're unacquainted with their work. I'm serious.

Outside, there were several people waiting for the bus. There were three benches; I noticed everyone was crowded onto just two. When I took a closer look, I discovered the reason why. Huge splotches of fresh blood decorated the third bench – red on white. I was repelled as much as anyone else, and then I started to wonder how the blood got there. My bet is that it was from a nosebleed. Whether spontaneous, or from a smack on the beak, I couldn't tell. Maybe it was a stab wound. I love those experts in 'blood-spatter evidence' you see on TV. Sorting this scene out would be child's play for one of those guys.

On the two benches was an interesting assortment of humanity. There was a ruddy, chatty, good-natured couple from Sydney, Australia; they seemed stereotypical to me, likely on their way to meet their mates Bruce and Sheila at a pub. There was a friendly, stocky black lady heading home to South Carolina. There were also two young Swedish women on holiday who looked great and spoke idiomatic English. Are Scandinavians *born* speaking perfect English?

Speaking of speaking, there was also a tall, slim, well-dressed man with an English accent. I am fascinated with the different regional English accents, and this guy spoke upper-crust, southern, plummy, posh, *BBC English,* otherwise known as *Received Pronunciation, or R.P.* He sounded effortlessly superior.

The group had begun to discuss the British Monarchy from respective points of view. The Aussies were stoutly against it; I was mildly in favor, for reasons of stability and tradition. The Englishman smoothly interjected that he had, as a matter of fact, danced with none other than the 'Queen Mum,' some years ago. He referred, of course, to Elizabeth Angela Marguerite Bowes-Lyon (1900–2002), the mother of Queen of Elizabeth II. This was at a function, he explained, put on by the Chancellor of the University of London, where he is a semi-retired professor of international relations. He said the admirable woman was a pretty fair dancer, especially in light of her age and the fact that she had been drinking champagne all evening. The good professor was on his way to a conference in San Antonio on International Affairs and popped down to Key West overnight for a quick look.

He and I sat across from one another for the four-hour trip up to the Miami airport. He was an amusing fellow; he amused himself, I thought, slightly more than those within earshot. He would tell a sophisticated story and then laugh uproariously at his own wit and erudition. Among other things, he related how the driver on the way south announced that the lavatory on his bus was to be used solely for purposes of urination. Pardon me? I really didn't believe him, but he seemed dead serious. I'd love to see how they enforced that one – perhaps by means of an electronic sensor, or highly-trained sniffer dogs.

He was a likable chap who spoke of many things. His daughter is a GP in the south of England. A bit later he imparted the following tidbit: in the city of Oxford is an extraordinary spot called Parson's Pleasure on the River Cherwell. There, faculty members are often seen taking the air in a state of complete undress. My eyebrows shot up.

These freewheeling dons, he explained, can often be seen by

passing punters on a summer's day. The more modest of these libertines use the pages of the *Times* (the *Oxford Mail* in a pinch) to create a private shadow. This seems quite out-of-keeping with customary Oxford behavior, as I imagine it, but it does give you an idea of what goes on below the stuffy surface of things. I wonder if C.S. Lewis or Lewis Carroll ever went there. I later learned that Parson's Pleasure was closed in 1990; this is a great pity.

My companion said his "speciality" – not specialty, mind you – was Africa. He is regularly summoned, so he claimed, to Chatham House, the London think-tank to formulate government policy in this regard. That sort of work, he said, is full of headaches; this statement surprised me not at all.

His first name was Frank; his surname, and I swear it's true, is a synonym for *toilet*. This must have incited much jocularity as he made his way through life. I wonder what the Queen Mum must have thought. We discussed national senses of humor, and we agreed, jokes don't travel or translate very well. He says the main trait of British humor is *sarcasm*.

My own sense of humor seems somewhat skewed in that direction, and a few people have rebuked me for it. In my own defense I mildly point out that if you check the etymology of sarcasm (and one certainly *ought* to do so), you find it concerns cruelly tearing out a chunk of *muscle*. I intend no such injury; therefore, I reason, I am definitely not sarcastic. Satirical, sardonical and ironical are nearer the mark, if you ask me. I don't want to hear any more about it! Case closed.

Frank gave me a real-life example of something he found amusing. He had turned his car the wrong way into a one-way street in London. He was stopped by a policeman on his beat; one imagines the bobby flagged him down with his night-stick. The policeman said, very politely, "If I might make a suggestion, sir: perhaps an appointment with your optician might be in order."

Frank broke into gales of laughter which turned a few frizzy heads his way.

The English are certain their humor is the best the world. I perused a book on British humour (sic) not long ago. In the preface the author asked the rhetorical question, "Where would we Brits be without our superlative sense of humour?" His answer was, "Germany."

I thought it was a terrific joke at the time – my apologies to those who disagree.

Frank was great company, and I was sorry when it was time for us to part; we said good-bye at the Miami airport. That proves it again: there's simply no telling who you'll meet on the bus.

During my short wait in the tiny Greyhound depot in Miami, one fellow-traveler caught my eye. He was wide-eyed, and paced restlessly about the waiting area, muttering to no one in particular. Mutterers drive me crazy. He was worked up about the price of his ticket that was "ninety bucks and should have been seventy."

Honestly, he looked like he'd just escaped from a local institute for the criminally insane. He sat facing me at a distance of about a yard. I could smell his breath and see the small veins in his bulging eyes. I was just wondering what might happen next, when the young fellow sitting next to him asked him what he was talking about.

He answered, "Oh, I'm just talking gibberish." For a raving lunatic, I though the remark quite insightful. After that he settled down a bit.

When I'd boarded the express service to Orlando I noticed a couple of unusual travelers. One, a skinny fellow of about 50, got on with what looked like a huge bag of laundry. He had an odd arrangement of hats, about three I would say – all on his head at the same time. His clothing was remarkably clean, and I thought I could smell fabric softener. Of course he was 'plugged-in,' listening to his favorite tunes. He was pretty uninhibited; he started waving his arms around like a madman, and then he started singing dreadfully off-key. For a while be played air-guitar for all it was worth. He was totally unselfconscious, as though he was sitting in his own living-room.

After a while he pulled out a printed form; I strained to see what was on it. The only word I could make out was *Furlough* on the top line. Later he pulled out a red plastic card with the words *U.S. Department of Justice* across the top, and his photo on it. My bet is that he was a cheerful new parolee who had just cleaned himself up at a laundromat and was heading off to see his sweetie.

Then there was a suave young black man, with what looked like entirely golden teeth – up and down. I was so intrigued I thought of asking him about them. I thought briefly of impersonating a dentist, so as not to appear too nosy. Unfortunately he got off before I had a chance.

My seat-mate for this segment was a young black man, very fit and well-dressed. For a long time he had his earphones in, and I thought, at this rate I was never going to make his acquaintance. However, after a while I saw he was actually on his phone. They were discussing things concerned with cars – maintenance, oil and the like. After he hung up I asked him if he was having car problems. He readily answered my question, and we fell into animated discussion for perhaps two hours.

He was 28, married, and had a daughter who had just turned one. He was bright and articulate, studying marketing at a college in Orlando, where he lived in an extended-family situation that included his parents-in-law. It was a happy arrangement, he said. His mother-in-law was remarkable in the fact that she was 'The Apostle' of a church called The New Majestic Temple of Faith. He was originally from Jamaica, but emigrated with his parents, brother and sister when he was seven. His people, he said, were from hard-working stock and had no time for laziness, dishonesty or excuses. Unfortunately his parents separated and his father, with whom he is still in touch, lives in Maryland.

One of the things we talked about was how to approach the world of investing. I gave him some tips that I believe will help him and his family. I love to see ambition in young people, and especially in ethnic groups with historic economic obstacles.

He said that he realized success was up to himself, and no amount of grousing about the 'weak economy' would do. He said, weak economy or strong, it was up to himself to 'make it.' He also had discovered that self-discipline was essential to the life he wanted for himself and his family. He was in the process of setting up a business the nature of which I didn't quite grasp, but he was certainly committed to it.

His wife and daughter met him at the depot in Orlando. He introduced me warmly. It was a touching moment; I liked them very much. I wished them well, and we parted. The next day I flew home to the bosom of my dear family.

PART THREE

The Road to Salt Lake City

left home on a wet Friday morning in April. The delta of the Fraser River was a study in soggy drabness: vast fields of standing water – grey, black and brown. It might have been wishful thinking, but for a moment I thought I saw a slim streak of blue sky in the distance.

Much has been thought and written on the subject of *water,* and I find the topic and its ramifications fascinating. Certain personalities can be described in terms of water. My daughter, for instance, is like a placid lake: untroubled, fresh, and clean, happy to be where she is. My son, on the other hand, has the nature of a river: restless, rushing, swirling, moving in a certain direction, touching many places and people in the process. Myself, often I feel like water behind a dam, pushing, pent-up, fit to burst out. Setting out on a journey opens the floodgate for me; the feeling of freedom and joy is enormous. But you know that already.

Still on the Fraser River Delta I noticed many places of worship of Asian origin: Buddhist, Hindu, Sikh, Muslim... no churches, mind you, but numerous temples and mosques. It simply shows that human beings from everywhere have a strong religious impulse, one that they bring with themselves when they move to another land. It's clear to me that the search for *truth* is much less compelling, provided that one's 'religious niche' is comfortably occupied.

I'm very interested in bus drivers. Who are these people who choose a job that involves transporting perfect strangers here and there, day and night, rain or shine to thousands of different places? If the profession didn't actually exist, it would seem implausible to me. Most bus drivers I have known personally are of a decidedly philosophic nature. The work is *essential*, which results in a sturdy self-respect, while at the same time it's straight-forward, which allows plenty of time for contemplation. I have two bus-driving friends, for example, who have advanced theological degrees, and love the opportunity that driving gives them for prayer, and occasionally ministering to the spiritual needs of the passengers. They do this every day.

As we zip along I'm reading George Orwell's *Down and Out in Paris and London,* which I find very funny, especially his description of the filth and chaos of running a restaurant in post-WWI Paris. His comments on the "elaborate caste system" in a restaurant are especially interesting. If anyone considering a career in the restaurant business were to read this book, my guess is he'd do an immediate about-face. Orwell also describes poverty in a way that is anguishing and repellent – no romance about it, except in retrospect. His description of what a diet of bread and margarine does to a man's body and soul is unforgettable.

I've rediscovered Orwell recently... what a writer! His style displays clear thinking, and his choice of words is, I believe, *perfect.* I've also recently read his essay *Politics and the English Language.* He is merciless in his criticism of woolly thinking and sloppy wording, which, he points out, go hand-in-hand. More than this: one is the cause of the other.

According to my sources, his two best-selling books (*1984* and *Animal Farm*) outsold any other two books by any other author in the 20th century. It is sometimes noted that he was 'the best-selling novelist of the 20th century,' which is far from true – he's not even in the top forty, because other novelists have published far more titles. I'm horrified to relate that the top two best-selling novelists of the 20th century are Danielle Steel and Stephen King.

There goes civilization.

On we plunged into the wet streets of Vancouver. At the north end of the Burrard Street Bridge are situated innumerable tall apartment buildings. This is one of the last places on Earth that I'd want to live. Awful, cloned, soul-less monstrosities that look as if they were designed by a nasty little boy with a vast Lego set. You couldn't pay me to live there.

We passed a venerable old stone church tucked in among the office towers, shops, eateries and hotels. It was *Christ Church Cathedral*, looking as ectopic as an outpost of an alien galaxy. There were big signs on front and rear of the building, evidently left over from Easter, proclaiming, *Alleluia* – something I imagine would be lost on the average passer-by. Next door is a shopping plaza, Cathedral Square, in which there is a store with the odd name The Black Goat, possibly, I imagined, an emporium of Wiccan paraphernalia. The sight suggested spiritual dissonance to me.

The main bus depot in Vancouver is a cavernous place, and has a wonderfully old-fashioned feel, like the railway station in the 1945 movie *Brief Encounter*. The most arresting thing about it is entirely unexpected; it is the piped-in music in the lavatory. The acoustics are magnificent there, and the music fairly ricochets among the fixtures, floor and ceiling. The choice of music, moreover, is astonishingly high-brow – I heard *Jesu, Joy of Man's Desiring; Claire de Lune; Bolero*. I hated to leave. I asked the attendant, a young Filipino, about this and he says the security staff chooses the selections. If I'd had time, I would have tracked down the fellow responsible and praised his good taste. This is truly one of the great lavatories of North America – there's little to compare with it, I imagine, this side of Vienna.

In due course, we left Vancouver, headed for Seattle, a familiar route. I had been talking to a man from Powell River.

"I'm going to visit my brother in Seattle – he's real sick," he said, "Cancer."

He was a tall gent about seventy, rather stooped, using a cane. His right foot turned in and didn't support him well. He had a big shock of hair, rather like the Beatles, but dyed an unlikely copper color. He was reasonably friendly, about five out of ten, I'd say. He seemed pained.

There was the usual rigmarole at the border, and in fact two of our company were not allowed to continue with us. When we reached Bellingham, a bunch of us went in to use the facilities. I followed the man with the Beatle haircut in using the urinal, and to my horror, discovered he'd left a pool of blood right there in the drain – all over the deodorizer puck. My guess is that he was quite ill himself and going to visit his brother for the last time.

I'd recently bought a small battery-powered Grundig radio and I had brought it along on this trip. I was surprised what a pleasure it was – to be moving along in comfort, while listening to a variety of high-quality, absorbing programs on NPR. *All Things Considered* with Robert Siegal and Audie Cornish especially stands out in my mind; this show is produced for the evening commute, and is consistently rated one of the most popular radio shows in the country. Sad to say, it's not nearly as popular as *The Rush Limbaugh Show,* which, in my view, is a serious abuse of freedom of speech, one that sets my teeth on edge.

National Public Radio was established by the *Public Broadcasting Act* signed by President Johnson in 1967; broadcasts began in 1970. I've always loved the network for its inspired blend of news, commentary, culture and bull's-eye humor. Both *Car Talk* and *Wait, Wait, Don't Tell Me* are clever and charming.

As I listened I learned, for instance, that both George W. Bush and Donald Rumsfeld can't visit certain European countries – they didn't say which – because they'd run the risk of being arrested as war criminals. The announcer talked of how dubious the Bush administration's ethics were, noting that the new Bush "*Lie*-brary" was soon to open in Dallas. I could scarcely believe my ears. They noted with some concern that this particular library was "unlikely to be very popular."

I believe these presidential libraries are essentially monuments to past presidents rather than a place you can borrow a book if you have a card. If they do lend books, the overdue fines must be astronomical. Perhaps the fines are collected by the Secret Service – at ungodly hours. I imagined being awakened at two in the morning by a heavy knock on the door....

Later, as we surfed along the highway, I saw a hand-lettered sign on side of road, standing crookedly off by itself, announcing the availability of *HAMBURGER* somewhere nearby. An arrow indicated the direction in which those interested should hasten in order procure such a rare comestible. I wonder how that sharp marketing idea is working. If it does work, the proprietor may put up another with *HOT-DOG* written on it. At that rate he'll be able to retire in no time.

Nearby was another sign, hanging precariously from a rusty chain, twisting in the wind. It was in front of a shuttered motel indicating that the management would be *Back in 2010.* That was fully three years past. The owner was apparently an optimist, but somehow must have tripped up. I'd love to know what became of him.

As I browsed the *Bellingham Coffee News* I saw a quote that I found intriguing, which rang true: "It is only in sorrow that bad weather masters us; in joy we face the storm, and defy it." This bit of wisdom is from one Amelia Barr. I'd not heard of her, but I liked the quote and decided to learn something about her.

She was an English-American novelist, the author of some eighty books; she lived between 1831 and 1919. She was evidently greatly accomplished at overcoming adversity. In her own life she somehow weathered the death of her husband and three of her six children from yellow fever when she was 37 years old; she went on to gain acclaim as a writer.

When she was seventy, she wrote a book on the subject of *success,* containing nine laws she had herself discovered, and enthusiastically adopted. I think they're marvelous, and so reproduce them here, in her own words.

1. Men and women succeed *because they take pains to succeed.* Industry and patience are almost genius; and successful people are often more distinguished for resolution and perseverance

than for unusual gifts. They make determination and unity of purpose supply the place of ability.

2. Success is the reward of those who "spurn delights and live laborious days." We learn to do things by *doing them. One of the great secrets of success is "pegging away."* No disappointment must discourage, and a run back must often be allowed, in order to take a longer leap forward.

3. *No opposition must be taken to heart.* Our enemies often help us more than our friends. Besides, a head-wind is better than no wind. Who ever got anywhere in a dead calm?

4. *A fatal mistake is to imagine that success is some stroke of luck.* This world is run with far too tight a rein for luck to interfere. Fortune *sells* her wares; she never gives them. In some form or other, we pay for her favors; or we go empty away.

5. We have been told, for centuries, to watch for opportunities, and to strike while the iron is hot. Very good; but I think better of Oliver Cromwell's amendment – *"make the iron hot by striking it."*

6. Everything good thing needs time. Don't do work in a hurry. Go into details; it pays in every way. *Time means power for your work.* Mediocrity is always in a rush; but whatever is worth doing at all is worth doing with consideration. For genius is nothing more nor less than doing *well* what anyone can do *badly.*

7. *Be orderly.* Slatternly work is never good work. It is either affectation, or there is some radical defect in the intellect. I would distrust even the spiritual life of one whose methods and work were dirty, untidy, and without clearness and order.

8. Never be above your profession. I have had many letters from people who wanted all the emoluments and honors of literature, and who yet said, "Literature is the accident of my life; I am a lawyer, or a doctor, or a lady, or a gentleman." *Literature is no*

accident. She is a mistress who demands the whole heart, the whole intellect, and the whole time of a devotee.

9. Don't fail through defects of temper and over-sensitiveness at moments of trial. *One of the great helps to success is to be cheerful;* to go to work with a full sense of life; to be determined to put hindrances out of the way; to prevail over them and to get the mastery. Above all things else, be cheerful; there is no beatitude for the despairing.

So believed the mature Amelia Barr; I'd love to have known her.

By nightfall, we arrived at the Seattle bus depot in the driving rain – "just chuckin' down" as an old English friend of mine used to say. As usual, the place seemed like an underfunded cross between a mental asylum and a refugee camp. One good thing though, because it functions as an unofficial homeless shelter, they let *anyone* use their lavatory. Some depots do not allow this; you need to have a bus ticket. In terms of ambience, it's pretty much at the opposite end of the spectrum from the Vancouver facility – no fancy music, for sure.

I was hungry, so I donned my foul-weather gear, deployed my umbrella and ventured forth to see if I could find something to eat. Dark, cold, rainy… who in their right mind would live here? I took shelter in a tiny grocery and bought two bananas for a dollar.

Back outside, I kept on looking. I entered a sub shop, selected a table, unburdened myself of my dripping luggage and umbrella, and placed my order, all the while afraid to turn my back on my belongings. The only two other customers were well-dressed young Moslem women speaking, as I imagined, *Urdu.* What on earth were these sophisticated women doing here? I wondered. I later learned the answer; they were waiting for *their* bus. I'd love to have learned something about them. Where had they come from? Where were they headed? How did they take the execution of Osama Bin Laden?

Back I went to the depot. Paul Theroux, who has traveled the world by every conveyance including dog-cart, doesn't think much of bus stations. In his *Ghost Train to the Eastern Star* he writes, "…bus stations the world over are dens of thieves, cutpurses, intimidators, mountebanks and muggers." Obviously, I don't agree, but I myself may be a mountebank, for all I know. Bus stations are a glorious hodge-podge of humanity all right, entirely unadorned, and therefore of great interest. A bus station is never the same twice, and if my own experience is any gauge, really nothing to worry about. In fact, I recommend them: the lowly bus station is a real look into the lives of people you would probably never meet anywhere else, and being in one certainly sharpens one's perceptions.

I looked around the place. High on one wall was a small television tuned to CNN. The current international worry was to do with the lunatic North Korea regime of Kim Jong-un, spoiling for a fight – threatening to destroy its neighbors – and the U.S. – by nuclear means. I think it was JFK that cautioned against getting sucked into conflicts that, if ignored, would eventually blow over. In today's world, when crises come thick and fast, it's good advice.

Two of the denizens of the depot caught my eye: a middle-aged man with a tiny head, traveling with his elderly mother, and an emaciated man with severe Tourette's Syndrome who looked like he was just killing time till morning. He grimaced and twitched continually.

By ten o'clock I was on my way southeast. I was glad to be rolling again; I'd had my fill of the depot, the rain and the neighborhood. On way out of town a huge fuzzy red neon sign in the far distance proclaimed, *WONDER BREAD.* What? I had heard that manufacturer had gone under, a victim of changing taste in bread. Modern folk do prefer real bread over sliced white goo. Who is looking after the sign, paying the electric bill? This is the sort of thing that presents itself for leisurely consideration when you're riding the 'Hound.

So I took it upon myself to learn something of this product. It's quite a history. *Wonder Bread* was originally produced by the Taggart Baking Company of Indianapolis in 1921. The new brand was named by vice-president Elmer Cline, who was inspired by the International Balloon Race recently held in his city. Perhaps he was easily amused, but apparently old Elmer was filled with 'wonder' by the sight of myriad multicolored balloons, and thought such a thing had big commercial potential. Thus, in one stroke, the brand name and the logo sprung fully-fledged from Elmer's fertile brain.

By 1925 Wonder Bread had become a national brand; "It's Slo Baked" became its curiously dull motto. In the early thirties Wonder managers decided to *slice* their product before shipping it, heralding the practice as "the greatest forward step in the baking industry since bread was wrapped." Many customers considered this move heretical; others feared the bread would be stale by the time it got to them. Slicing was, in fact, suspended from 1943–45, due to a shortage of steel, but this much was clear: sliced bread was a great thing, and here to stay. It was a writer at the *Kansas Star* that came up with the expression "the greatest thing since sliced bread."

During the forties the federal government became concerned about the poor food value of manufactured bread – roughly that of wallpaper, I think. Accordingly, authorities mandated the addition of certain vitamins and minerals to white flour, a measure known as *enrichment,* or *fortification.* These are indeed *powerful* words and must have done wonders for sales. The enrichment process produced what was termed the 'Quiet Miracle' – the reduction in the incidence of certain vitamin deficiencies – no small thing.

So as not to weary the reader, I'll skip over the rest of the *Wonder* story, including the *Howdy Doody* connection. Suffice it to say, that by 2012 the thrill – the *wonder* of it all, shall we say – was gone, and the company stopped production in the U.S. I'm happy to report, however, that those interested in purchasing *Wonder Bread* can still do so in two countries. In Canada it is produced by the *The George Weston Company* of Toronto; in Mexico it is produced by *Grupo Bimbo* of Mexico City. Here and there, the wonder continues.

After rolling along for a while, the driver felt inclined to make an announcement. A propos of nothing, he said he wanted to give us some advice about odors of "human origin." He told us to do our utmost to keep our "odors down" when we use the toilet, and to take care not to waft our foot odor around too much. He actually said it is a *federal law* not to remove your shoes on a bus. I must remember to consult an attorney on that one, when I have time on my hands.

Can this be true in a country where you need not trouble yourself to wear a helmet when riding a motorcycle, guns are everywhere and the buses have no seat belts? What would be the penalty for removing your shoes? A fine? Hard time? Community service, maybe, or probation? Legislators' time would perhaps be better spent – for a start – by *mandating seat belts* in buses, as is the case in more civilized places.

The driver's name was Kurt or Curt, a name that suited him perfectly. I imagined his parents were retired concentration camp guards, Ernst and Waltraut Brunner, now living in a deluxe nursing home in a leafy suburb of Buenos Aires. Young Kurt must have had a rough upbringing. He treated his passengers like so many inmates.

At a break at a truck-stop in Ellensburg, Oregon, he read us – in stentorian voice – a section of what I call *The Greyhound Riot Act*. He told us not to wander off, and if we did, he wasn't prepared to take the trouble to track us down. If we weren't back on the bus in ten minutes – *too bad* for us. "After all," he said, "the logo on the bus is a *grey*hound, not a *blood*hound" – quite admiring his own wit. He obviously says that every trip. It was a snotty remark that didn't endear him to anyone aboard. It was dark then, and I thought I heard him slapping his leg with a riding-crop.

And speaking of "reading the Riot Act," I wondered where that strange expression came from. I have heard it all my life, and always thought it had something to do with quelling riots and dispersing mobs. That's pretty much it. In fact, *The Riot Act* passed by the British Parliament in 1714 authorized local law-enforcement to declare any group of twelve or more to be unlawfully assembled and to require their dispersal on pain of penalty. The complete title of the legislation was *An Act for preventing tumults and riotous assemblies, and for the more speedy and effectual punishing of the rioters.* Rioters were given an hour to disperse.

I picture some boozed-up miscreant yelling, "What's the bloomin' rush?" Any stragglers were guilty of a "felony without benefit of clergy, punishable by death"!

I had never spent the night on a bus and thought it might be an interesting thing to do. Not only that, but staying on the bus all night gets you to your destination faster, and saves having to spring for accommodation and a daily onward bus ticket. So it was that a handful of us were deposited with little ceremony at a truck-stop – the Pilot Travel Center, to be precise – in Stanfield, Oregon at two in the morning. I had to wait, Kurt said – with an unmistakable touch of sadism – "about 40 minutes" for the next bus to arrive.

After bidding so long and good-riddance to Kurt, my mind strayed to thinking about the place I happened to be standing at that moment. I think "24/7" truck-stops don't get the respect they deserve.

These places are beacons of light, hope, warmth, food, tools, conversation and help of all sorts. I wondered, who chooses to work there? Are they lost souls? Thank goodness for these places, in any case. Where else are you going to go between two and three in the morning when you're on the road between buses? Think of it – they *never, ever* close! To my mind, it's a glimpse of eternity, seen through a glass darkly.

One commentator wrote, "The historic image of the truck stop is somewhat shady to some people, and make no mistake, any place that is open for business 24 hours a day is going to attract its share of interesting characters... .Many truckers drive what amounts to an apartment on wheels. Sleepers, electricity for crock-pots or hot-plates, Internet access, satellite TV – all the comforts of home right there

in the truck...... there are barber shops, showers, business centers...
Internet lounges, movie theaters, places to get your rig tricked-out
with chrome."

I got to thinking: how long have these unlikely places been in
existence? Well, if you're interested, it all started in the forties when it
became necessary to have diesel fuel available for truckers doing long
hauls on state highways. In 1956 President Eisenhower established
a national highway system by way of the *Federal Aid Highway Act.*
Over succeeding decades, the Dwight D. Eisenhower National System
of Interstate and Defense Highways was constructed; this naturally
spurred the trucking industry immensely.

In 1948 Fred Bosselman, a part-time farmer and trucker, opened
the Bosselman and Eaton Truck Stop in Grand Island, Nebraska. It was
quite an innovation, but definitely a timely idea. As trucks got bigger
and more numerous, so have truck-stops. In 1965 old Fred opened the
Bosselman Truck Plaza, billed as the *truck-stop of tomorrow.* I was
happy to learn that the Bosselman family business continues to thrive
to this very day.

There are about 20,000 truck stops in the country. Most now, however, call themselves *Travel Centers;* the snooty ones are called *Travel
Plazas.* I dislike the word *plaza*; it seems to cheapen anything it describes. Who finds a toll plaza appealing? Some of the worst hotels
and malls I know have *plaza* in their names – almost a guarantee of an
irritating, dispiriting experience.

Using the word is a futile attempt to make the tawdry seem ex-
otic. You've got your Plaza Cinema, your Shopping Plaza, your Civic
Plaza, your Olympic Plaza, your Plaza Library, your Toyota Plaza,
your Scotia Plaza, your Plaza Games, your Plaza Magazine, your Pizza
Plaza – enough already! I always thought it meant a *place* in Italian.
Not so – it's from the Greek, meaning *broad street.*

The signs of these truck stops shine forth into the night – visible
from space, no doubt – proclaiming: *TruckStops of America, Flying J,*

Roady's, Love's, Dixie Travel Plaza. The world's largest truck stop is the *I-80* in Walcott, Iowa – an immense place that, by the way, hosts the Trucker's Jamboree each July, with irresistible events such as the Super Truck Beauty Contest, and the Iowa Pork Chop Cook-out. I may see you there one day, as I pass through.

At about three I wandered into the restroom. Something fixed to the wall caught my eye. It was a vending machine that had the look of a medicine cabinet. Across the top was emblazoned *Health Mart,* in reflective letters. Because health is my business, I approached with interest. It was, in fact, a dispenser of rubber products of a prophylactic nature – condoms and assorted erotica – with names that would make a goat blush: *Glo-Boy, Midnight Stalker, Thriller, Herbal Tickler* and my personal favorite, *Rainbow Lolly.*

The price for such wonders of health-enhancement was surprisingly modest, a mere seventy-five cents, taxes in. For the same price you could get a mysterious *Pandora's Box,* filled with a dozen erotic delights, a description of which was not forthcoming. *You'll want 'em all*, the sign assured.

This leads the mind naturally to the topic of truck stop prostitution, a subject of which, I'm happy to say, I have no first-hand experience, or otherwise. I'm told truck-stop prostitutes are known as *lot lizards*, which does make the mind reel a bit. Sociologists tell us the prevalence of truck-stop prostitution is highest near large cities. Some wag has likely dubbed these places 'trick stops.'

The Vince Lombardi Truck Stop on the New Jersey Turnpike has a reputation for the most aggressive roadside prostitution in the country. I'm guessing the old coach – a devout Catholic, by the way – would be dismayed. For further reading on the underbelly of life on the road, see John McPhee's fine book, *Uncommon Carriers.*

I wandered around the lot scanning in all directions for the next bus. I wondered what would happen if I missed it... would I have to spend 24 hours here waiting for the next one? Could I perhaps pick up some work – maybe as a greeter? I was pacing around the spot at which I supposed the bus would arrive, hoping to get the *rear* seat, which could accommodate four posteriors of ample size. I was, of course, planning to stretch out on this couch-like arrangement and sleep most of the way to Salt Lake City. This seat's proximity to the toilet didn't bother me a bit.

A snatch of an old Allman Brothers song occurred to me at that instant:

> *My daddy was a gambler down in Georgia,*
> *Wound up on the wrong end of a gun,*
> *And I was born in the back seat of a Greyhound bus,*
> *Rollin' down highway forty-one.*

On the leg of my journey from Seattle to Stanfield the back seat of the bus was entirely occupied by a hefty young black woman with a buzz cut, who seemed to enjoy the privilege immensely – flipping, flopping, now prone, now supine, up on one elbow, sighing with pleasure. She looked daggers at anyone who approached.

Unfortunately, the same woman was waiting for the same bus as I was. I was determined to get that position at all costs; I was a seat-predator, ready to pounce. When I bounded aboard, what should I see? To my dismay, nay *devastation*, it was the self-same big broad, reclining with abandon upon the seats of my desire, like she owned the thing! For practical purposes, indeed, she did.

The only way she could have done this is to have flagged down the bus at the top of the parking lot, and scampered aboard an instant before I did. I had been outflanked, outwitted, outclassed; this woman was a consummate traveler, a bare-knuckles Greyhounder. She'd earned her stripes and was entirely deserving of such an upgrade. I took off my hat to her, and she smiled knowingly. I checked on her periodically during the next few hours; her sleep was, as Proverbs says, *sweet*. In fact she looked like she was under general anesthesia. I felt a fatherly urge to tuck her in. I look forward to matching wits with her again, one day.

I wondered idly if Greyhound had a loyalty rewards program, with points that could be redeemed for certain exciting goods and services. They could offer admission to special ritzy lounges at select bus depots. How about priority seating, extra leg room, fully-reclining seats, pretzels, beer? They could call it the *Greyhound Gentry Group* ('3-G'). I'd join up for sure, as long as they would guarantee me the back seat, and no fooling about it.

Our new driver's name was Deanna. I liked her instantly; she was polite, cheerful and clearly enjoyed her work. She told good jokes. Moreover, she treated the passengers with frank respect as though her livelihood depended upon us – an alien concept to most Greyhound staff. The fellow behind me said to no one in particular, "The cops in Vegas are real lenient, but cops in Utah are assholes."

I made a mental note.

Sitting near me was a black woman of about thirty who was traveling with her son, a lad of ten – a handsome and polite little fellow. Her main feature was a *mountain* of hair… worlds, galaxies of it. It reminded me of a huge woolly UFO. The term *Afro* doesn't begin to do it justice. She changed seats every so often; she sometimes sat just in front of me. When she reclined her seat, her hair advanced into my personal space to the point where I thought I might sneeze. The pair kept to themselves, but I somehow surmised they were heading for some place in Texas, a fact I found amazing. It wasn't the destination that was so odd, but the fact they were riding the bus clear from Seattle to Texas, a journey that would take about three days. This mother and son were clearly made of stern stuff.

No opportunity arose for casual conversation until I saw the little fellow munching something from a bag. Our eyes met.

"Whatcha eatin'?" I asked.

He didn't answer directly, but smiled and asked, "You want some?"

"Sure, please," I said – just to be polite, delighted to have made some human contact. They turned out to be a horrid salty snack called

Chester Fries – red, crooked cylindrical things. He reached his little right hand into the bag, pulled out a bunch and extended them towards me, across the aisle. I reached out with my left hand and took them. I munched them while making appreciative sounds.

"Pretty good," I said, smiling. Something passed between the three of us that I found entirely touching.

He asked me if I wanted more; I said, "Maybe later, thanks!"

Among the travelers was a black gent heading, he said, "to Vegas." He sat many rows behind me. He had a mellifluous voice; he might have been an announcer, or a singer. I'll call him 'Mel' because his voice was unusually *smooth* like that of the American jazz singer, Mel Torme – the 'Velvet Fog.' It makes me feel short of breath when I think of him.

At one point Mel began a monologue that went on for ages. The acoustics in the bus made me think of the Whispering Gallery in St. Paul's Cathedral where a whisper against the inside wall of the dome is clearly audible to an ear inclined toward the dome on the opposite side, a great distance away. In the 'Hound, it's the same sort of thing: you have simply to speak toward a window, and bingo! Everyone on the bus can hear it clearly, even if they're wearing earphones or earplugs. I'm not sure of the physics involved, but I can tell you I got sick of listening to him drone on. One pointless story blended with the next.

At one stage Mel told a complex tale of what happened when he lent his "ID" and car to a friend named LeRoy. It seems LeRoy had had his license suspended for an unspecified infraction, but nevertheless, "LeRoy had a hot date and needed wheels," was how Mel put it. Accordingly, off sped LeRoy with Mel's car and ID, happy as anything, for a night on the town with his dolly. Hey – what are friends for?

If I understood the account correctly – and, believe me, I was not trying – LeRoy was detained by the police and, not wishing to disclose his own identity, naturally used Mel's ID. This seems like a hopeless gambit to me, but that was the best addle-headed LeRoy could do. It

wasn't long before police deduced they'd arrested someone other than
Mel. So before the night was out, both Mel and LeRoy were, legally
speaking, in pretty hot water.

Forgive me, but I must have dozed off about then, no doubt missing
some key events of the story, such as what penalties were meted out.
In any case, my bet is that, because of these shenanigans Mel was riding the 'Hound instead of styling along in his own car. This byzantine
story, in all its dimensions, took fully half an hour to relate, and bored
me silly. Mulling over this nonsensical account, it occurred to me that a
national DNA database may be in order; it would sort these fellows out
just right, and would certainly avoid any vagueness about who's who.

Every so often when zipping down the highway on the bus one
must use the lavatory. As a rule, the Greyhound biffies are not too bad.
They are reasonably well-maintained and contain only three things: a
giant porta-potty, a roll of entry-level toilet paper, and a wall-mounted
dispenser of alcohol-based hand sanitizer. The toilet is full of a mysterious blue fluid with lumps in it, sloshing around like mad. The door
is usually an awkward rig that folds in the middle with much creaking
and popping. Most of these doors are bent somehow, and you're lucky
to find one that actually locks. Often you have to do your business
while holding the rickety door closed with a hand or a foot. No one
actually tries to get in, because everyone saw you heading in there in
the first place.

On the way back to my seat I saw something I'd never seen before:
a woman sitting *backwards* in her seat; her back was against the back
of the seat in front of her. With legs crossed, lotus-style, she looked
pretty comfy. I guess she was hoping the person in front of her didn't
feel like reclining, or perhaps she just pushed back. It was surely odd
to see, and got me thinking about all the positions it's possible to assume in a bus seat.

As I've mentioned, in the U.S. one is unconstrained by a seat belt,
which allows assuming any number of contortions. In all, that night I

think I slept five hours. The most comfortable position for me was to have my head against the right side of the bus, lying on my right side. My legs stretched into the aisle (another federal offense, I'm told). My right leg went under the armrest, my left over it. It's interesting to spend one such night, but I'm not keen to repeat the experience any time soon.

Shortly after daylight we rolled into Twin Falls, Idaho. Through bleary eyes I saw some poor soul in a cow suit, standing on her back legs, waving a big sign that urged *Eat More Chicken!* What? Was that a hallucination? Would we next see a huge chicken promoting the consumption of beef?

The rest of the morning – involving brief stops at Burley in Idaho and Tremontin and Ogden in Utah – sadly must remain shrouded in obscurity; I can't remember a thing about them. I do know, however, that by mid-afternoon on Saturday, the bus reached Salt Lake City, where I hoped to spend a couple of days. I planned to look into the Mormon view of life.

I walked through back streets to my hotel. On the way, I noticed a prominent billboard lamenting that Mr. Obama had won the recent election. The sign hinted the result was probably contrary to the will of God. The sign advised folks to *'Above all, guard your pensions.'* I found it a curious sentiment.

Early next morning – Sunday – I went out for a ramble around downtown. Salt Lake City to me has a strange feel to it – not disagreeable, just an oddness, as if it was built by aliens straining to make the place look like a normal American city. The streets are incredibly wide, the buildings imposing. All was clean and orderly; there were hardly any pedestrians; the place looked sanitized. The SLC police must have quiet time of it. My skin tingled; I thought I must have stepped through a *portal*, straight into somewhere else altogether. The place feels extraordinary, perhaps paranormal; it's hard to explain.

If a city has a particular nature, I would Salt Lake City's is that of *pride*, verging on smugness. It is likely so because of what its Mormon founders and their successors have achieved – a big, prosperous city where 150 years before was empty desert. From this inauspicious beginning these sincere souls have built a mammoth religious organization that now spans the globe. Their achievement is all the more remarkable because of the opposition they encountered from the mainstream Christian church, which they had profound doctrinal differences.

A few words about Mormon history are in order.

In a nutshell, the church was founded in 1830 by Joseph Smith of upstate New York as a result of certain alleged experiences. Smith believed he was appointed by God to renew the church of Jesus Christ. In order to do this, and to establish Smith's authority, the body of Holy Scripture needed to be amended. Thus, an angel appeared to Smith and led him to some hidden gold tablets, which the angel proceeded to translate into English for him. This translation became *The Book of Mormon*, which gives an account of early American history and Christ's involvement in it.

Smith and his followers met with considerable success in the early years of the church. Eventually, however, largely due to the church's practice of polygamy, the group met with vigorous persecution in New York. After being driven out of New York, they were hounded – from New York to Ohio, then to Illinois and Missouri. In 1844, Smith was arrested in Carthage, Illinois and charged with 'conspiracy.' An armed mob stormed the prison and Smith was killed in the firefight. He was 38.

(A note of clarification about polygamy: the more exact term is *polygyny* – the practice of a man having more than two wives. The practice was banned by the main branch of the church in 1890.)

A succession crisis ensued, resulting in the appointment of Brigham Young as prophet and leader. It was Young who led the largest part of

Smith's adherents – by then known as *The Church of Latter-Day Saints* – to the Utah Territory, then part of Mexico.

Many parallels exist between the Mormon exodus and that of the Children of Israel, with whom the Mormons strongly identified. Both the Mormons and the Children of Israel fled persecution at home in order to settle, after innumerable trials, into their 'Promised Land.' Accordingly, Young was venerated by many as a 'Mormon Moses.'

Young and his followers arrived in Salt Lake Valley on July 24, 1847, a date now recognized in Utah as Pioneer Day. A mere month after arriving in the valley, Young founded the Mormon Tabernacle Choir. Over the next two decades, more than 70,000 Mormon pioneers crossed the plains and settled in in the area. This energetic and persistent group and their offspring later established hundreds of settlements in the western states, Canada and Mexico.

I was amazed to learn that Sir Richard Burton, the great English explorer, ethnologist and author traveled to SLC in 1860; his aim was to conduct an inquiry into the 'religious life' in the area. Burton was a top-notch adventurer; he makes me think of the thrilling novels of H. Rider Haggard I read as a lad – and, of course, Indiana Jones, who was basically a take-off on Haggard's hero, Allan Quatermain.

Burton captured my imagination. In 1853, with astonishing ingenuity and dash, he slipped undetected into the holy city of Mecca – the first European to do so in 200 years. He really did his homework before setting out – learning languages, mastering the art of disguise, being circumcised(!) and so on. As a non-Muslim, had he been caught, he would have been executed in an imaginative manner. However, he was indeed not caught, and related his adventures in *A Personal Narrative of a Pilgrimage to Al-Medinah and Meccah*, published in 1855.

Burton was also a tremendous linguist; he knew about thirty Asian, African and European languages, plus many dialects. One of his more unpredictable accomplishments was to translate the *Kama Sutra* into

English, and to have it published. I'll bet he had fun with that. It is said that his "tone ranged from the jocular to the scholarly."

According to my sources, Burton traveled to SLC by 'coach.' When I heard this, I felt an instant kinship with the man. Had he come a hundred years later, he may well have arrived on the 'Hound. Ah... Sir Richard Francis Burton, KCMG, FRGS – what a guy... surely, a man after my own heart. What a seat-mate he'd have been!

Continuing my exploration of Salt Lake City, I noted a great many large buildings concerned with the world of finance. The Merrill Lynch Bank, for instance, is on South Main Street, and is as grand as the Vatican. I was puzzled, though, because I'd heard ML had gone under not long ago. As it turns out, ML was bought out by the Bank of America in 2009, during the Great Recession. From then on, Merrill Lynch has been the name of the investment banking and wealth management division of the BofA. ML manages a tidy $2.2 trillion in client assets, and is the largest brokerage firm in the world. In downtown SLC, this fat corporate pussycat fits right in.

Another larger-than-life edifice is the Grand America Hotel, also on South Main Street; I read somewhere that it is the "finest hotel in the country," although I have no idea how they go about choosing among top contenders. I checked with *Travel and Leisure* magazine, and the Grand America doesn't even make the top twenty. Nonetheless, the place *is* really spectacular. This astonishingly grandiose building was built and owned by the late Robert Earl Holding, who was born in 1926 and died, oddly enough, a few days after I visited the city. I deny any causal link. He was born in SLC; his parents are described as 'apartment caretakers' and, naturally, were Mormons.

Holding was a consummate entrepreneur, starting with nothing but intelligence and desire, and ending up with an empire comprised of – but not limited to – the Sinclair Oil Corporation, numerous hotels, an immense cattle ranch in Wyoming and two ski resorts. When he died, he was worth $3.2 billion, which made him the 155th wealthiest person in America, according to *Forbes.*

The 775-room Grand America was built in 2001, at a cost of $185 million. It was built just before the 2002 SLC Olympics. The hotel's facade is comprised of twenty-five-ton granite slabs quarried in Vermont; Holding personally selected them. I have visions of slaves towing them to Utah on rollers. A mirror in the lobby, I'm told, cost a million dollars. The hotel motto (are you ready for this?): *Taste is Grand.* I bet it cost them a bundle to come up with that bit of brilliant self-puffery.

Isn't it in horrid taste to exalt one's own taste? Since when was *excess* considered good taste? A smidgen of restraint might not go amiss at the Grand America. In human terms, think of the difference in attitude between Donald Trump and Warren Buffet. Give me the *Sage of Omaha* any day of the week.

The more I thought about this stuck-up place, the more it got on my nerves. One of the marvelous things about travel these days is the ability to get unbiased hotel reviews from Internet sites like *Tripadvisor. com.* Reading scathing hotel reviews is great fun. The bumbling apologies of the hotel managers are especially amusing, to the effect, "We're not sure how THAT could EVER have happened at OUR hotel! We are looking into your concern, to ensure it NEVER happens again. We hope we have the pleasure serving you again in the near future." Fat chance.

Former guests at the Grand America are wonderfully candid – some are brutal. Many of their reviews are hilarious: they talk of "robotic staff... clenched smiles... creepy Stepford-like service... the fake-friendly manager." And then there was the guy who said he couldn't get service even if he'd set himself on fire, and so on. All this joy for $200–$600 a night! From other comments, I gather GA staff is not in agreement with the consumption of alcohol or coffee; according to the online reviews, their service, portions and prices make this quite plain.

All this walking around town was making me mighty hungry, so I began searching for a place to get breakfast. It sounds easy, but I soon discovered that all nearby restaurants were closed for the Sabbath; they had signs on the doors that said so. What was I to do? I reckoned I'd better head in the direction of my hotel and check opportunities in that neighborhood.

Choice was sharply limited, but I did find one place willing to feed a hungry infidel. It was, in fact, Denny's, that paragon of American cuisine, home of the mighty Grand Slam breakfast. Now the Grand Slam is probably the greatest agglomeration of cholesterol that can fit on a plate. Nevertheless, it is, I declare, sublimely delicious, so I ordered one, straight-up, without a qualm.

In minutes I could feel strength surging through my frame like a rising tide. Morbidity and mortality statistics aside, in some ineffable way this kind of grub just has to be what body and soul need sometimes, to offset the rigors of the road.

I knew Denny's has been part of the travel landscape in America for as long as I can remember, but I'd really not thought much about it. It's one of those places you take for granted – always there, always open – like a hospital. Denny's is the place many of us wouldn't be seen dead in in our hometown, but when we're 'away,' it'll do fine.

Snobbery aside, I've looked into Denny's and have found some things of interest. First, I'd like to congratulate them for using an apostrophe on their signs. There are not nearly enough apostrophes on the signs of the nation; Denny's is doing its part to address this regrettable sloppiness. This outfit operates over 1,600 eateries in the U.S., Canada, Latin America, Japan, New Zealand, Qatar and the United Arab Emirates. Denny's is a huge American multinational corporation – and more power to 'em, I say.

Denny's was founded in in 1953, in Lakewood, California, by Richard Jezak and Harold Butler. The original name was Danny's Donuts, but a few years later was changed to Denny's to distinguish itself from a competing chain called Doughnut Dan's. Don't you just love the imaginative names? Its head office is now in Spartanburg, South Carolina. Spartanburg, by the way, has the nick-name 'Sparkle City'; its curious motto is, 'Always Doing.' Spartanburg, by all appearances, has no time for idlers.

Denny's was a winner from the start, and by 1981 there were 1,000 restaurants in all 50 states. The iconic Grand Slam was born in 1977. Icons come and go, but the Grand Slam's popularity is undiminished, no matter what else may be going on in the world. Come war, plague, famine, floods, 9/11, earthquake, economic catastrophe, you name it – the Grand Slam stands tall, a beacon of stability and deliciousness. Seriously, though, how hard is it to present pancakes, eggs, bacon, sausage and hash browns on one plate? I could have thought of that.

A couple more odd things about Denny's might interest you. On the positive side, Denny's is the largest corporate sponsor of Save the Children, the venerable charity championing children's rights in developing countries. Not so laudable, however, was a huge judgment against the company in a 1994 class-action racial discrimination lawsuit. Denny's was found guilty of multiple cases of discrimination against certain Afro-American customers, and was fined $54.4 million. The price of discourtesy is high.

Back to breakfast: as luck would have it, I had arrived during a special Denny's event called Baconalia. As far as I could tell, it's a celebration involving putting bacon into every dish, and a veritable orgy it was. This phenomenon, this total bacon-mania, may be a function of the current glut of pork in America, but in any case, it is a mighty threat to cardiovascular health and must be the perfect terror of the porcine community. One imagines herds of swine fleeing from persecution, four-legged refugees in search of better prospects abroad. If this profligate Baconalia keeps up, the pig may go the way of the dodo.

In any case, you could scarcely order a thing in this restaurant without a wagon-load of 'crispy' bacon either in it, on it, or under it. Now I like bacon fine, but with all its fat, nitrates and carcinogens

– there is a limit. I was truly stunned and repelled when I saw you can order a Bacon Maple Milkshake, or its companion dish, The New Salted Caramel Brownie Sundae with Bacon. This, I submit, is a perfect example of too much of a good thing.

Like most of us, I have eaten bacon all my life, without having given it much thought. I knew, of course, it came from pigs, but I hadn't bothered to learn how it's actually made. When I was a child, I presumed it was basically strips of pigskin, rather like what they make footballs from, only salty and fatty. I decided to research the subject – to obtain carnal knowledge, you might say.

The essence may be condensed in a couple of paragraphs. The word itself is derived from the Old High German *bacho,* meaning *buttock.* So far, so good. The USDA defines bacon as 'the cured belly of a swine carcass' – mouth-watering prospect, to be sure. Bacon has been described as the National Meat of America. When traveling in Britain, one is expected to gobble down a bacon-laden 'Full English [or Scottish or Welsh] Breakfast'; same thing in Ireland. Future anthropologists will likely implicate bacon in the decline and fall of Western civilization.

Bacon is prepared from different parts of the beast. In the U.S. the main source of bacon is from the belly. This is a rather fatty product, known as *streaky bacon* and is called *American style bacon* outside the country itself. In most other countries, however, the sides and the back of the animal are used, which give a much leaner product. In Jewish and Muslim areas, where, of course, eating pork is forbidden on religious grounds, a product called bacon is prepared from the meat of other animals such as goat, lamb and chicken.

In the U.S., bacon made from the sides and back is called *Canadian bacon*; in Canada, it's called *back bacon* and in the U.K., it's simply called *bacon.* To my taste, British bacon is best. The Brits even make sandwiches out of it. I had a bacon sandwich at a B&B in Hereford once that I've never forgotten. I ate it waiting for the bus to Hay-On-Wye.

The pork meat is first cured in strong brine. During the brining, certain other agents are added – sodium nitrite, saltpeter, vitamin C, sodium erythorbate – to accelerate the process and to impart color. The result is called 'fresh' or 'green' bacon. Thereafter, it may be dried in cold air, or it may be boiled or smoked. Boiled bacon, I'm told, is ready to eat – as is most smoked bacon. Hey, take my advice: cook the stuff yourself; it's unhealthy enough without picking up a tapeworm in the bargain.

We have to admit it, bacon is *addictive*. How can that be? The reason, it turns out, has been determined scientifically. Bacon contains several tastes which flavor experts call *umami*. These are substances that impart a unique flavor to a certain food, a "high flavor profile" that's instantly recognizable, and for which there are few substitutes.

There is easy money in this. In his book *The End of Overeating*, Dr. David Kessler notes the common restaurant practice of jazzing up a dull dish by "throwing cheese and bacon on it." It works every time. I'll bet that a rolled-up copy of *The Salt Lake Tribune* with bacon and cheese would be a big hit at Denny's. Certain diners would likely prefer it flat, like a stack of pancakes.

Now I could go on about the food and drink that has been bacon-flavored (e.g. vodka, chocolate, mints), but I can't stomach thinking of these perversities. Bacon flavoring, I was astonished to learn, is not a new thing, but has quite a history. In his 1708 satirical poem *The Sot-Weed Factor,* Ebenezer Cooke complained that practically all the food in America was 'bacon-infused.'

I thought I'd have a little fun with the waitress, so I asked her about these bacon-enriched dairy delights.

"How are they, actually?" I asked, straight-faced, like I was a columnist for *Bon Appetit*.

"Oh," she said, giving her gum a few chews, "they're *real* good… the bacon tastes just like… pecans."

I thought about this for a moment; then I asked if I could possibly get a substitute for bacon in a sundae – chunks of nice organ meat – kidney, liver, brains, perhaps. Well, at this point, she guessed she was dealing with a wise-guy and she wasn't one bit amused; it was like I was mocking something dear to her heart. She rolled her eyes, drew back her lips exposing horse-like incisors, and just walked away, tossing her frizzy red hair as she went. She must have been sick of bacon jokes. Give me real pecans any day.

I finished my Grand Slam and prepared to leave when a fellow-diner caught my eye. He was a young man of about twenty, sitting alone; by my reckoning he weighed 500 pounds. His enormous girth was swaddled in a black T-shirt with the puzzling words *Honey Badger Don't Care* printed on it. He was drinking a Coke; I wondered if it was Diet. His hair was slickly moussed and neatly parted in the middle. My mind crowded with questions. Who was this man? Why was he so big? What did the T-shirt slogan mean? Where do you get big shirts like that? Was he a nihilist? What did he dream of? Where's he off to after breakfast?

Sadly, I'll never know, as I decided to respect his privacy. But I wished him well in my heart, and left.

My main motive for visiting SLC was to learn something of what the Mormons were about. I'd known a few in my time; one of the brightest students in my med school class, to the bemusement of many, became one after graduation. It is the fourth largest denomination in the country, and, much more robust and organized than most of the others.

Mormonism had been getting enormous publicity in the previous year. Mitt Romney lost the election partly because many Christians voted against him on religious grounds. I needed to look into Mormonism; who are these people, what do they believe, and why? I decided to walk up to Mormon headquarters on Temple Square, about a mile from my hotel. As I walked along, I was again struck by the cloying eeriness of the place, like nowhere else I've ever been. I looked over my shoulder, and quickened my pace.

I looked ahead and saw a basket of red flags fixed to a streetlight post. It took me a second, but then I realized what they're for: pedestrians are supposed to carry these flags to enhance visibility when using the crosswalk. It struck me as a terrific idea. At the same time it occurred to me that maybe carrying a flag is the way the authorities keep track (by CCTV or satellite) of who's crossing the street, and what they may be up to.

And speaking of crosswalks, I've long been skeptical of their usefulness. Of all the pedestrians I've ever heard of who were killed by motorists, most have been struck in a crosswalk, smack-dab in the middle, as a rule. Think of it like this: the car is the bullet, and the pedestrian is the poor critter in the cross-hairs. It's like walking across a shooting gallery. A feeling of safety while in a crosswalk is pure delusion, and therefore, for my own safety, I assiduously avoid them; I'm serious. This is something that has worked for me all my life. So far, I've never been injured crossing the street, not so much a scratch.

This crosswalk talk naturally leads the mind to the topic of *jaywalking*. What is it exactly? What kind of a goofy word is *jaywalk*, anyway? Is it illegal everywhere? Who is prosecuted, and what's the penalty? Being a helpless victim of overzealous curiosity, I just had to find out.

There is much to learn when one delves into the subject. I have, for instance, learned that jaywalking is illegal across the country, and has been so for many decades. Enforcement is desultory, however, often only triggered by repeated complaints from drivers about pedestrian behavior in a particular part of town.

The first known reference to jaywalking was in December, 1913, says Peter Norton, history professor at the University of Virginia, and author of *Fighting Traffic – The Dawn of the Motor Age in the American*

City. That month, a department store in Syracuse hired a Santa Claus who stood on the street with a megaphone, bellowing at people who didn't cross properly and calling them 'jaywalkers.'

The Santa used a slang term for a gullible, empty-headed chatterbox, something like a blue-jay, known for its impertinence and lack of sense.

The history of jaywalking is full of odd events. In 1923, certain public-spirited worthies in Cincinnati had become alarmed at the number of pedestrians hit by speeding automobiles. Accordingly, they circulated a petition demanding the auto industry limit the speed of its cars to 25 mph; 42,000 people signed.

As you might expect, this outcry caused the auto industry to become, shall we say, *defensive.* The Auto Industry Safety Committee mounted a press campaign arguing that pedestrians themselves were to blame for being hit by cars. (To me, it's like saying a person who gets shot is at fault for putting himself in the path of the bullet.)

Once this idea was firmly planted in the public mind, auto lobbyists moved to 'stage two' of their plan: they set up safety programs with the ostensible aim of protecting schoolchildren. Their rallying cry was, in effect, "The streets are full of cars, so the children need to watch out." Consequently, anti-jaywalking laws were adopted in many cities in the 1920s; they became the norm in the 1930s. Thus the auto industry slyly sidestepped the responsibility of producing cars with speed governors designed for use on city streets.

Local attitudes toward jaywalking are perfectly obvious when you walk the downtown streets of any city. In some places I've been – Boise, Idaho springs to mind – people are utterly compliant with the signals. You'd think it was a capital offense to jaywalk. You find the opposite in London, where pedestrians ignore crossing signals, flooding into the street with seeming invulnerability. Vehicular traffic meekly yields. It's weird, but it works. Were jaywalking an Olympic event, Londoners would walk away with all the medals.

However, lest you think Londoners flout traffic laws in general, I must caution you. Special crossings do exist, with cute names like *Zebra, Pelican* and *Puffin*, which are, unaccountably to me, strictly observed. Clearly, the British, a sturdy and individualistic race, subscribe to Emerson's idea that "a foolish consistency is the hobgoblin of little minds."

I'm not sure of the statistics, but I'll bet pedestrian injuries in London are proportionally rarer than in Boise. Here's how I see it: when crossing the street, you simply have to keep your eyes open and your wits about you. Period.

Before we flog the subject to pieces, here's something I found amusing: in Singapore, signs prohibiting jaywalking show a stick-man walking with one foot in the gutter and one on the sidewalk. Isn't that marvelously inscrutable? Knowing Singapore, the penalty is probably caning, or a stretch in the slammer.

I arrived at Temple Square, the city's focal point, just steps away from the financial district. The square was dominated by the Temple itself, a fantastical thing that looks like one of those synthetic-historic buildings in Las Vegas, like the Hotel Excalibur, with a touch of Disney thrown in. Atop the steeple stood a golden effigy of the angel Maroni, complete with trumpet.

The angel himself – described as 'dignified and neoclassical' was of course the one who helped Joseph Smith translate the gold tablets that became the basis of *The Book of Mormon*. The statue is twelve feet tall, made of copper overlaid with 22-karat gold leaf. It was set in place in 1892; today it looks *brand new*.

The Temple, I was surprised to learn, is closed to the public, and church members do not talk openly about the rituals that take place within. The church holds that the temple and its rituals are *sacred*, and not actually secret, but rather *private*. They maintain that early Christianity had similar practices and bodies of knowledge that were kept quiet to preserve their sacred nature. This sounds like cultish nonsense to me.

I felt like a visiting alien, as I walked the grounds surrounding the official buildings – the Temple, the Tabernacle, the Assembly Hall, the Visitors' Center, and Museum. The whole place was spotless, and humming along to its own extraordinary rhythm. It was a sunny day, just after noon. Many young, earnest-looking folk were chatting and eating lunch on the grass. The men and boys wore white shirts and dark, thin ties; the women and girls wore summery dresses. Gender ambiguity, it appears, is unknown here.

To my mind, the typical Mormon man has a certain look to him. It's like he stepped out of the early sixties. He is slim, clean-cut, wide-eyed, and wears horn-rimmed glasses. He has, I would say, a *neutral* facial expression, almost a mask. The glasses reminded me of Clark Kent; many of these lads looked rather like CIA rookies from, say, 1963.

Probably the weirdest thing about what was going on was a broadcast over the public-address system. It was a constant monologue, at moderate volume; though I tried to grasp what was being said, it made no impression on me at all, except that it was an impenetrable bore. I suspect it was someone reading from one of their holy books. In any case, no one seemed to be listening; the voice droned on; people ate their sandwiches, talked, or dozed in the sun. The people on the grass seemed like fodder for an enormous, wealthy system mainly concerned with *conformity* in thought, word and deed. I got the distinct impression that independent thinking would be discouraged, perhaps *rooted out*.

The disembodied voice put me in mind of Orwell's *1984* where the author describes the telescreen, a surveillance device installed by the State in every room of the nation. This appliance had two purposes: first to broadcast ceaseless propaganda in support of the regime, and secondly to monitor what went on in every room in the country. The following excerpt will give you an idea:

> *Inside the flat a fruity voice was reading out a list*
> *of figures, something to do with the production of*
> *pig-iron... the young and pretty women ... were the*
> *most bigoted adherents of the Party, the swallow-*
> *ers of slogans, the amateur spies and nosers-out of*
> *unorthodoxy....*
>
> *It was terribly dangerous to let your thoughts wander*
> *when you were in any public place or within range of*
> *a telescreen. The smallest thing could give you away.*
> *A nervous tic, an unconscious look of anxiety, a habit*
> *of muttering to yourself – anything that carried with it*
> *the suggestion of abnormality, of having something to*
> *hide. In any case, to wear an improper expression on*
> *your face... was in itself a punishable offense. There*
> *was even a word for it in Newspeak: facecrime....*

All in all, my experience in Temple Square gave me the jimjams. During the recent Presidential election campaign, the Mormons attempted to persuade the public that theirs was a legitimate Christian denomination, not too different than the Methodists, say, or the Presbyterians. Accordingly, I took it upon myself to do a pointed study comparing major features of historical Christian teaching to those of the Mormons. Many of the differences I found stunning. Annotated source material can be found at www.cultwatch.com/mormonism, and is true to the best of my knowledge.

For instance:

- Unlike Christianity, Mormonism teaches that there is not one but many gods.
- Jesus was married (at Cana).
- Jesus and Satan are brothers.
- Individual salvation is exclusive to the Mormon Church.

- Heaven for a Mormon woman is to be eternally pregnant, populating her husband's own planet.
- The Mormon God is an exalted man from a planet near the star-base Kolob (wherever that may be!)
- Joseph Smith called Christian beliefs "an abomination."

I also did some digging concerning what happens when someone defects from the Mormon fold. I was amused to see *Newsweek* calls this phenomenon 'when the saints go marching out'; it's also called 'going PostMo.'

Certain ex-Mormons are making it their business to rescue others from the organization. A support group of many hundreds calling themselves the SLC PostMos meet twice weekly at Kafeneio, a coffee house in downtown SLC. When a Mormon defects, the church disciplinary counsel has the right to 'excommunicate' that person, and to forbid contact with any other active LDS members. In a state where over sixty percent of the population and nearly eighty percent of Utah politicians are Mormon, you can imagine the courage it takes to make this step, and the feeling of isolation that commonly results. Many have to leave their jobs with Mormon-owned companies. I understand Utah has the highest rate of clinical depression in the country, and the seventh-highest suicide rate.

This suggests that many are bound to the organization by *fear* – fear of ostracism and, it must be noted, of *eternal damnation*. This fear, this terror, is, of course, what lies behind such rigid conformity. One ex-Mormon cult-buster put it this way, "People intuitively know that first and foremost their primary identity is as a nameless soldier in the army of Mormonism." Another said, "Leaving the church is almost like going into the witness protection program."

Well, that was enough for me! On the basis of what I learned in Salt Lake City, I declare there is *zero* chance that I would ever enlist with the Mormons, although I do subscribe to many of their values: independence, family, thrift, industry, shirt and tie, clean living, horn rims, and so on. But I find their spiritual beliefs and heavily-enforced conformity entirely unappealing.

All this gawking and walking about had given me quite an appetite, so I decided to search out somewhere to eat my evening meal. I guess I'm a bit of a creature of habit, but in any case I took myself in the direction of Denny's, a place for which I'd developed a certain fondness.

I must say something about the street names in SLC. They are crammed with numerical and directional data. Now I readily admit that numbers aren't my strong suit, and I have a horrid sense of direction, so the street names made my head spin. This is just one more reason I'll not likely return to SLC.

The first incongruity I noticed is that the streets with *south* as suffix, run east and west. And similar with the other cardinal directions. I tried so hard to grasp the system. I even read about it a couple of times – I practically blew a fuse. I'm not sure if the following is an actual address, but it seems to me that a certain address might be expressed: 127 *NW South St E.* What on earth is one to make of that? For me to master the system would be like gaining a working knowledge of the language of another planet – maybe *Kolob.* I've got other plans.

I noticed a couple walking on the sidewalk ahead of me, dressed as if they had just been to church. The man was short, and his trousers were at least six inches too long, gathering in heaps on his shoes. He was in his seventies, and had perhaps shrunk in height over the past couple of decades. My theory is, that he thinks of himself as being as tall as he ever was, so he buys his trousers accordingly.

I caught up to them at a crosswalk. They spoke pleasantly to me, "Live here, do you?" the man asked.

They were from Ventura, California and here to attend a national convention of their church. I kept my views to myself; we chatted a bit and parted amicably.

I was getting hungrier all the time. After a long trudge in a hypoglycemic fog, I fairly staggered, salivating, into Denny's – as visions of Seniors' Spaghetti and Meatballs danced in my head.

As I waited to be seated, I overheard someone shout, "What do you mean, you're out of spaghetti and meatballs… *and* ice cream?"

The waitress replied, "I'm sorry, sir, we're just fresh out…."

Her voice trailed off. This struck me as bad news indeed; even though I was starving, I seemed to be starving for spaghetti and meatballs in particular. I stayed long enough to hear the exhausted waitress explain that there'd been a "big convention in town" and the conventioneers – a ravenous lot, I imagine – had stripped the restaurants clean. I thought of a plague of locusts partial to spaghetti, meatballs and ice cream – porky little blighters.

I quickly formulated a Plan B. I had spied a Subway restaurant nearby, and I knew they had a terrific meat ball marinara sub. It took me five minutes to get there. There was a young Hispanic man behind the counter; the place was otherwise empty. I placed my order for a Footlong, which I knew contained eight succulent meat balls, among other tasty ingredients.

There was a pause, and the fellow said, "Say-nyor, there is a slight problem." My throat tightened.

He explained that because of the "beeg con-benshong" there were but four meat balls in the house. No matter… believing half a sub is better than none, I asked him to prepare a *six-incher* – six full inches, mind – and would he be kind enough to so without delay. It was though I was in a Monty Python sketch, something along the lines of *The Cheese Shop*.

I'm happy to say, sustenance came in the nick of time. Thirty more seconds and I would have convulsed and slipped into an irremediable coma. Seldom have I enjoyed a meal so much; scarcity intensifies the enjoyment of even ordinary things, including the lowly meat ball.

The next morning I was back at the Greyhound Depot – address

300 S 600W – see what I mean? I had somehow torn my trusty umbrella and as I waited for the bus, I set about repairing it with needle and thread. I derive a perverse pleasure doing something no one else on Earth is doing at a specific point in time. I venture to say, no one in any of the world's thousands of bus depots was repairing an umbrella at that instant. I sat next to an old woman who looked like a Mexican farm worker; I half-expected her to give me some pointers on the stitchery, or at least raise an eyebrow at such an odd sight. I was amazed; she seemed not to notice me at all. She stared straight ahead. What could be going on in that brain of hers?

Once I'd finished the repair it was time to board the bus. That day I'd planned to go to Las Vegas to meet my friend Wally and proceed to explore northern Arizona. SLC was a real eye-opener for me and I was glad for the opportunity to study this odd place and its mentality. But I was eager to get out of town.

I felt the old joy of the road rising up in my heart, as in a cloud of gritty dust, we pulled out of the station.

PART FOUR

A Taste of the Mississippi

'd been laid up for nearly a year with severe back pain and, at the worst of it, I didn't think I'd ever be able to travel again – certainly not solo. However, after many months of intractable pain, I had a major operation that turned out to be a complete success. I came out of the anesthetic, and the pain that was like a crocodile's jaws locked onto my right buttock for months – was gone. About the first thing I thought about post-operatively was getting back on the road, preferably by bus. You do understand.

I've long had an urge to explore the Mississippi River Valley. I'm not sure exactly why, but it probably had something to do with reading Mark Twain when I was young. The Mississippi seems to me *America's River* – a country in the *form* of a river. Thoughts crowded my head as to the points of interest along the way. For months before I left, I pored over maps and read as much as I could cram into my poor old brain. Think of it! The Civil War, riverboat gamblers, commercial shipping, fishing, civil rights, literature, music, food… a universe unto itself. I felt like embracing it all, crazy as it sounds in retrospect.

As much as anything, Paul Robeson's sublime version of *Ol' Man River,* from the musical *Showboat,* drew me in that direction; I just had to head down that way. Robeson's character, a slave named Joe, longs to escape his wretched life picking cotton in fields overlooking the river. He was stuck – as much as if he was tethered to the very spot – but the river, seeming to mock him, just kept rolling along. The sheer *heart* of the song drew me to that valley, and made me want to meet the magnificent *Ol' Man* himself.

This is the verse that did it for me:

> *He don't plant taters,*
> *He don't plant cotton,*

And dem dat plants 'em is soon forgotten,
But Ol' Man River,
He jes keeps rollin' along....

I intended to go from the headwaters of the river in Minnesota, down-river through about ten states, dozens of towns and several big cities, until I arrived at the Delta, all in about two weeks. With any luck I thought I might make it to Pilottown, at the very mouth of the Mississippi. As it turned out, my goal was wildly ambitious; I really didn't have a clue what I was trying to do. That doesn't bother me, however, when I remember Michelangelo's prayer, "Lord grant that I may always desire more than I accomplish."

Having recently been through my medical trials – more like the valley of the shadow of death – I decided I'd take all reasonable steps to prevent a relapse. Part of this was to avoid arriving in a strange place after dark. Accordingly, instead of arriving in Minneapolis late at night, I decided to first fly to Phoenix, and then the next day skip up to Minneapolis, arriving about mid-day.

On the way to Phoenix from Vancouver, I passed through U.S. Customs and various layers of the Department of Homeland Security. Entering the U.S. has become a serious nuisance for regular travelers. As I waited to be screened, for instance, I saw officers prodding a wheelchair-bound lady of about 85 years into a full-body scanner. My blood boils at the thought!

Overhead was a huge photo of the Statue of Liberty. It made me nostalgic for what it's supposed to represent: the plaque on its pedestal reads,

Give me your tired, your poor,
Your huddled masses yearning to breathe free,
The wretched refuse of your teeming shore.
Send these, the homeless, tempest-tossed to me,
I lift my lamp beside the golden door.

These powerful lines, incidentally, are taken from a sonnet called

The New Colossus, by New York Jewish poet Emma Lazarus, who died at age 38, in 1887.

It was a weird juxtaposition, this manifest lack of freedom taking place under the gaze of Lady Liberty. This brought to mind what Benjamin Franklin wrote about those who would sacrifice freedom for security. He thought such people deserved neither. Incisive lad, was Ben Franklin.

I wondered if anybody had ever erected a Statue of Security. Then I thought, this has already been done many times, huge statues various dictators have built for themselves – representations of Orwell's Big Brother: Lenin, Stalin, Mao, Pol Pot, Saddam Hussein, Hafez Al-Assad, to name a few. As I write this, Robert Mugabe, Zimbabwe's pariah dictator, has ordered a thirty-foot-tall bronze statue of himself. This is being made by an army of metal sculptors in North Korea, and is to be delivered by ship in time for Mugabe's 90th birthday. Seeing that monstrosity is bound to give Zimbabweans' feeling of security a great boost.

Upon arrival in Phoenix I was picked up by the hotel shuttle van driver, an older Hispanic chap named Francisco, and a very pleasant and chatty fellow he was. I had heard there was a 'freeway shooter' active in the area. I thought I'd tempt fate and sit in the front seat. The authorities had yet to make an arrest, and announced there appeared to be a number of 'copy-cat shooters' at large, too.

I never heard how it worked out, but I did learn that the shooter was using a BB gun. This rather took the drama out of it for me.

The weather was perfect, but plenty hot. We whizzed by a sign that read, *Divorce $200,* with a phone number; this I thought was devilishly misleading. Next we whipped by a car wash called *Clean Freak,* which I thought an excellent and memorable company name.

I asked Francisco about the dust storms I'd heard about that are an occasional feature of Phoenix life. He said they can be terrifying, especially when they hit at rush hour and the visibility drops to zero. They are actually called by the Arabic name *haboob*, which I thought was very exotic. The word actually means *blasting/drafting*. It results from atmospheric changes involving wind and barometric pressure which creates a wall of sediment that can stretch for sixty miles and reach a height of several thousand yards. These things can approach as fast as a car, and arrive with virtually no warning. I like novel experiences, but if I have a choice, I'll give the haboob a big miss. The photos are terrifying, like a gigantic brown, fuzzy caterpillar rolling toward you, eager to snuff out anything in its path.

The Phoenix airport is called Sky Harbor International. What a terrific name for an airport. That name is surely the envy of many other airports – Mafia Airport in Tanzania, say, or Moron Airport in Mongolia, not to mention Useless Loop Airport in Australia, or Eek Airport in Alaska.

The only airport name that beats Sky Harbor for sheer fun is Batman Airport in Turkey.

I'm not actually on a No-Fly list at this moment, but I may be on borrowed time, mainly on the basis of the type of experience I had that morning at Sky Harbor. Everybody knows you're not allowed to carry liquids of more than 100ml through airport security. It has occurred to me this is just a ruse to get people to buy drinks at inflated prices when they're waiting at the gate. No matter.

I stepped up to the Homeland Security officer and showed my passport and boarding pass and she waved me toward the inspectors and their infernal scanners. Just as I was undressing for the inspection, I remembered I had a thermos of coffee in my carry-on bag. Imagine my chagrin; I did not want to lose my thermos, which I carry as a kind of talisman when I travel. It's even got my name inscribed on it, a gift from my wife.

So, I went against the flow of passengers back toward the passport-checker babe, expecting all the while to be cut down by a hail of bullets, mainly in the chest. Surprisingly, she was not that put out and told me to ditch the coffee in a waste container. Thus 12 ounces of steaming coffee went into a bin meant for dry refuse, but what's one to do? I retained my precious thermos.

I remember having to go 'back-through' security – for some reason I can't recall – at Ben Gurion Airport in Tel Aviv. They didn't shoot me there, either. I must be more careful; I can't get away with this sort of thing much longer.

As I prepared to board, I noticed a mural exalting Delta Airlines: *Looking over everything, nothing overlooked.* Would that it were true; though it sounds more like the Eye of God to me. Never mind, there's always some wise guy ready to skewer such vanity. There are tons of acronym jokes at Delta's expense, e.g.:

- Drunken Engineers Land Too Abruptly
- Don't Expect Luggage To Arrive
- Damaged Engines Limit Takeoff Ability

Belying the pessimistic jokes, the flight from Phoenix to Minneapolis was just fine. Sitting next to me in the exit row was a Minnesotan couple whom I'll call Bill and Mary. They are of Swedish descent, and decided some years ago to relocate to Carefree, Arizona.

Carefree… that rang a bell. I'd read about Carefree in a book called *1000 Places To See Before You Die,* by Patricia Schultz. The name of the town raised in me the suspicion that the residents have been heavily sedated – perhaps even lobotomized – a giant psychiatric experiment run by a shadowy branch of National Institute of Mental Health of Bethesda, Maryland. One street is called *Why Worry Lane…* seriously. The thought makes me flat-line. I'd sooner live in a town called *Careless…* bound to be more exciting.

I quizzed my seat-mates about Minneapolis. Based on previous visits, I had a favorable attitude toward Minnesota, and I told them so. The quintessential Minnesotan to my mind is Garrison Keillor – intelligent, literate, funny, creative – downright *cozy* to listen to, and to read. Bill said there's a state characteristic known as *Minnesota Nice.*

I'd never heard of this, so I did some checking. It consists of a "polite friendliness, an aversion to confrontation, a tendency toward understatement, emotional restraint and self-deprecation." I guess that's the kind of folks I prefer – pretty much like Canadians, I'd say. I was happy to be flying in.

I told them I wanted to stroll along the river and get a feel for it, get the smell up my nose, get some mist on my specs, that sort of thing. They suggested I visit Nicollet Island, right in the middle of the river. I decided to take their advice, as you will see.

Once at the baggage carousel, I encountered a terrific example of Minnesota Nice. As each bag appeared, a strapping middle-aged man in shirt-sleeves adjusted it so the handle was positioned conveniently for its owner to grasp. In all my born days, I have never seen such a small, thoughtful measure taken at a baggage carousel.

"Gee," I said to the man, "what a nice thing to do. I've never seen that before."

Without missing a beat or a bag, he replied, "Just a little something to make you feel welcome. Thank you for your business."

Truly, I thought: only in America – maybe only in Minnesota. I felt good all over.

Later, after I'd checked into my hotel, I went looking for a Denny's. I found one after walking a mile or so. The place wasn't crowded; I was shown to one of the many empty booths. In the neighboring booth, facing me, sat a solitary diner. Who is this guy? I thought. He was a pudgy gent with quite an appetite, judging by the way he vacuumed up his grub – a picture of total concentration. Perhaps a businessman far from home, missing his family and trying to fill the void with food. I figured the name might be *Earl*. Eventually, his platter licked clean, he transferred his enthusiasm to his smart-phone, which he studied as though attempting to discover the meaning of life. I tried to catch his eye, but to no avail; he was really engrossed.

Curiosity was getting the better of me. I'd finished my *Seniors'*

Hot Turkey Sandwich with Mashed Potatoes and Gravy, and not having much planned, I decided to see if Earl might be interested in a chat.

"How're you doin'?" I asked.

His head snapped up. "Good! How are you?" he replied with a quick smile.

"Right... me, too," I called back.

So far, so good. I wasted no time in asking him where he was from and what brought him to Minneapolis.

"I'm from Easton, Pennsylvania, and I'm here doing business for my company – it's called *Crayola,* you maybe heard of it."

"They were my favorite crayons growing up – great colors!" I said.

"Did you know that eighty percent of the world's crayons come from Easton, Pennsylvania?" he asked.

I sure didn't; I'm a crayon ignoramus.

This is one of the wonderful things about travel. It puts you in touch with people you'd never encounter at home, and draws your mind out of its habitual ruts, into worthy subjects you might not have thought of otherwise.

Well, who doesn't have fond memories of Crayola? When I was a kid, this was the upscale brand, leagues ahead of the anemic, brittle *Peacock* crayons. Your entry-level Crayola product was the eight-color flat box. Next was the sixteen-color one, and so on up the line, in multiples of eight. The upper-crust kids often had the sixty-four-count box – big as a brick. Half of those colors we thought were for wimps – periwinkle, apricot,thistle – but it did have a built-in sharpener, which I thought was very slick.

Earl proceeded to deluge me with details of his company, past present and future. His company was established in the early twentieth century by chemist-entrepreneurs and cousins Edward Binney and Harold Smith, of New York. Their company was called, logically enough, Binney & Smith.

Binney's wife, Alice, came up with the name *Crayola* by combining the two French words *craie* (chalk) and *olegineaux* (oily). Because the main ingredient in crayons is oil, Binney and Smith moved operations to the Quaker State, specifically to the town of Easton.

The most unpredictable thing in the history of Crayola is that Edward Binney was *colorblind*. This extraordinary fact seems to me to be about as likely as Stradivarius being tone-deaf – but there you are.

Before I leave Earl and Crayola, I need to add that this company also produces *Silly Putty*. Again, whose childhood memories don't include playing around with that zany stuff? The name itself is a stroke of genius... absolutely unforgettable. It's a serendipitous creation that turned up during research to produce a rubber substitute during WWII. Many silly things can be done with it, believe me, but its scientific definition is anything but: *It is a viscoelastic liquid silicone, a type of non-Newtonian fluid, which makes it act as a viscous liquid over a long period, but an elastic solid over a short period.* Now that's serious physics.

The definition does not hint at what fun it is; but we must move on. But I can't leave the subject before relating that Silly Putty was taken into lunar orbit by *Apollo 8* astronauts. One can imagine what they did with it in zero-gravity. Do I ever love trivia.

I enjoyed my chat with Earl and I think he was glad to talk with a curious foreigner about a subject dear to his heart. He loves his company and the joy it brings to the word. Who knows, tomorrow I may run into a sales-rep for Smith and Wesson. That would be a different kind of conversation altogether.

Not forgetting the focus of this account, I decided next day to ride downtown to meet the River. I was actually staying near the mammoth Mall of America, an institution that interests me not at all. In any case, I had to get there in order to catch a train downtown. Once there, I noted I had to take the Blue Line. Well, what a system! It's neat, clean, simple to navigate and cheap. The fare for seniors is 75 cents, and no one even checks your ticket. This is another marvelous example of Minnesota Nice.

After a dozen stops, I arrived at Nicollet Mall, which I figured had to be close to Nicollet Island, which had been recommended to me the day before by my seat-mates.

When planning this trip, I'd hoped to visit Hibbing, Minnesota, the childhood home of Bob Dylan, a great favorite of mine. Alas, Hibbing is north of Minneapolis, and the Mississippi flows south; I just wasn't going to get there. Imagine my surprise when I alighted from the train, to look up and see a gigantic, freshly-painted mural of Dylan himself. It was a triptych – with him as a young man on the left, middle-aged in the middle, and fully-seasoned and leathery on the right. It was extremely well-done and quite thrilling to behold.

It was painted over a period of two weeks by Brazilian artist Eduardo Kobra and his team of five. They painted twelve hours a day; the finished product is 160 feet wide and five stories high, and quite detailed – crow's feet, stubble, glint in the eye. It was completed September 8, 2015, just the week before. It's *magnificent*, everyone agrees.

I bounced along Hennepin Avenue, toward the bridge of the same name, which led to Nicollet Island. I was getting hungry and spied a Whole Foods Market on a corner ahead. I'd seen these markets many places before, but had never ventured into one, always imagining that I was too old and reactionary to feel at home there. Well, I got in there and couldn't make head nor tail of the place. It seemed like a re-education camp, more about the parlous 'state of the planet' than about groceries. I'm surprised there wasn't an employee at the door – a type of immigration official – to assess my political suitability. Frequently-ungrammatical signs trumpeted the party line:

- Eat Local!
- Eat Organic!
- Be Green-er!

- Use Only Recycled Hemp Bags!
- Reduce Your Carbon Footprint!

I imagine if I'd stopped exhaling I'd have drawn an appreciative crowd. At some point I stopped reading the signs; my visit to Whole Foods Market was an annoying and exhausting experience for me, a poor famished alien. Moreover, everything was ghastly expensive. I saw earnest young people queuing up at the salad bar. Each reverently held a recycled hemp tray in an attitude of prayerfulness. It reminded me of congregants taking Holy Communion – only they were helping themselves to what looked like compost at $9 a pound. The place got under my skin so much I left empty-handed, and still hungry, of course.

Many of Whole Foods' policies make sense, no doubt; I just really objected to being preached at when all I wanted to do was buy bread, cheese and an apple for lunch. I acknowledge that the fault is partly my own, but I did take pleasure in learning that Whole Foods has been in hot water with the Organic Consumers Association for selling GMO foods. What fun!

There was also trouble with the Departments of Consumer Affairs in California and New York because WFM overcharged on food sold by weight; the scales were systematically calibrated to the company's advantage. More like *Whole hypocrites*, I'd say.

I kept walking toward the River; I soon was at the south end of an impressive bridge. The Father Louis Hennepin Bridge of today is on the site of the *very first* span across the Mississippi, completed in 1855. I asked myself, who was this man, after whom many things are named in these parts?

Father Hennepin (1626–1705) was a Flemish Franciscan priest, missionary and adventurer – a man of great imagination and courage. He was part of a group commissioned by King Louis XIV of France to explore the 'unknown western' portion of the New World, and to locate the upper part of the Mississippi River.

In 1541, Spanish explorer Hernando deSoto was the first European to sight the lower part of this river in what is now Mississippi.

In 1679, the Hennepin party constructed the 45-ton barque, *Le Griffon,* and sailed west through the vast, uncharted Great Lakes. When they reached the northern part of Lake Michigan, they turned south. Near the south end of the lake they entered a river system that led, after some tricky navigating, into the Illinois River which flows southwest. Imagine their delight when, two hundred miles downstream, they slipped into an enormous waterway, flowing south. They correctly surmised that this was indeed the their goal and prize, the magnificent Mississippi River. All sense of hardship, fear and doubt were swept away in an overwhelming joy. These guys really had guts; they also had unshakable faith and incredible seamanship.

Shortly thereafter, Hennepin and his party were captured by a Sioux war party and held captive for several months. Eventually, they were given canoes by their captors, and they eventually reached New France again. Hennepin returned to Europe, and for reasons that may be imagined, was forbidden by his order to return to The New World. He probably had way too much fun.

By the way, Hennepin, I was surprised to learn, is credited for discovering two important waterfalls: *Niagara,* the most voluminous in North America, and the *Falls of Saint Anthony,* the only waterfall on the Mississippi, located just south of Nicollet Island in Minneapolis.

At the north end of the Hennepin Bridge I arrived at Nicollet Island, which, I must say, wasn't worth the effort. Maybe I somehow missed the main attraction, but I doubt it. Maybe I was still sour because of my Whole Foods experience. The Falls of Saint Anthony were right in front of me – surly, nothing to write home about. Walking opportunities are limited, and I was hungry and tired at that point. It was, however, moving to get my first glimpse of the River. At that location, I'd call its nature *stately.*

After that I decided on a random ramble through downtown to see what might perk me up a bit. I walked by a row of bicycles, part of what's called a *Bicycle-Sharing System.* We've all seen them in various cities and I always thought of the idea as cockeyed and bound to be a disaster. I ask, what keeps anyone with a hacksaw from stealing these things? What keeps low-lifes from stripping them, or selling them for scrap, or just wrecking them for fun? Do pedestrians walk around with helmets just in case they may use one? What if all the bikes end up all at the same place? Does a truck take them 'home' at night? Who checks the air pressure and lubes the chain?

I did enough online checking to learn that early attempts at these systems in Europe ran into a lot of theft and vandalism. In Amsterdam in the sixties, according to one source, "within a month most of the bicycles had been stolen, and the rest had been found in nearby canals." I rest my case.

Nevertheless, it is an appealing, if naïve idea, and cities kept trying to devise a bike-share system that works. With the use of CCTV, smart-phones, credit card deposits, fines, layers of IT and much police involvement, many of the weaknesses of the early schemes have been fixed. Such systems now exist in fifty countries; they are most popular in China, Spain and Italy. In the Chinese city of Wuhan, the most populous city in central China, there are 90,000 of these bikes.

I must say, for all the bikes I've seen sitting in racks, I've seen precious few actually being ridden anywhere. In Minneapolis that day, I did see one guy sitting on one – in its rack – while he jabbered on his cell phone. He was just taking a load off his feet, I'd say. The rack, incidentally, was full.

I was still hungry and kept looking for a suitable place to eat. I saw a sign in front of a pub: "The doctors were clear, you need more beer." It raised a smile, but I passed by. I saw a bearded man sitting on the sidewalk holding a sign that said *Stranded.* By the look of the tattered sign, he wasn't newly-stranded.

A minute later, I walked past a woebegone chap with a hand-lettered brown cardboard sign which read, *I need a cold beer*. I wonder if he's had any helpful responses. I attempted to catch his eye, but to my surprise and discomfiture, all I could see was the *whites* of his eyes. The effect was disturbing; I immediately thought of a zombie.

That naturally set my distractible brain off in the direction of zombies. They are seemingly very popular these days – you even see them in TV commercials, something I find perfectly revolting. Talk abounds on something called a 'zombie apocalypse,' whatever that may be. I think they must have taken over the spot vampires occupied in the public imagination until recently.

What on earth can be the popular appeal of this subject? I guess it's on account of a slews of zombie movies that have been made recently – 55 in 2014, alone. I asked myself, what is really known of these things? What are the hard data, if any? I worked for a time in Haiti and experienced a brush or two with Voodoo while there. Zombies are a prominent feature of Haitian folklore and are believed to be dead persons revived by the practice of *necromancy*. You may believe this or not, as you wish. The Haitian legal system, however, takes this seriously, ruling that if you drug someone into a 'lethargic coma, more or less prolonged,' you can be convicted of attempted murder. American anthropologist Zora Neale Hurston researched Haitian folklore in the 1930s and commented, "... if science ever gets to the bottom of Vodou in Haiti and Africa, it will be found that some important medical secrets, still unknown to medical science, give it its power, rather than gestures of ceremony."

The following morning I had to make it to the Greyhound depot. It was raining hard and I waited quietly in the hotel lobby for the shuttle. Near me sat an African-American woman who seemed to be waiting for something, too. And speaking of waiting, I've discovered if you wait for a stranger to start speaking to you, it can be a long wait indeed.

"Good morning," I offered.

"Pretty rainy out there," she replied with a polite smile; she was apparently on her own and seemed happy to talk. She was, she said, from Trenton, N.J. I'll call her Val.

"What brings you to Minneapolis?" I asked.

She said, "Why, I want to visit every state in the nation, and I've never been to Minnesota. I lucked-out – got a flight here for just $79."

"How many states to go? I asked.

"Let me see… I believe it's only eighteen now.

I expressed my interest and approval. I asked Val what she did; she said she works as an administrator for Medicare in New Jersey, plus she was a part-time pastor. We discussed medical things for a while, and then she asked me, "Where *you* headed, anyway?"

"Oh, I'm on my way down the Mississippi River," I said, trying not to seem too grand.

She wondered about my motivation. I explained it this way: some months before, I had seen Anthony Bourdain's TV show *Parts Unknown*, where he visited a particular modest restaurant in Jackson, Mississippi. It's called the Big Apple Inn and it's a great slice of local culture. The dish he most recommended was the pig's ear sandwich, served on a soft white bun, with plenty of hot mustard.

I said, "That seems like as good a reason as any for going down the River."

Well, to my surprise, this charming lady divulged that she had, in fact, been raised on a *Garden State* pig farm, and you could never get *her* to eat a pig's ear sandwich, no matter what – although her brothers did. I recalled vaguely that our vet forbade us giving pig's ears to our dear, omnivorous dog, Rosie. I may have to look into the matter a bit more, before I commit myself to such a sandwich.

Our young driver was a fresh-faced lad, very friendly and accom-modating. I was a bit surprised when he left the hotel before closing the rear door of the van, inviting the bags to tumble out willy-nilly along Route 35 W. Luckily someone noticed before disaster ensued. He told me he was heading for law school, and I wished him well. I felt like ribbing him about the door, but I held my tongue and am glad I did.

Val and I parted at the rail station, she to hit the Mall of America, I to make it downtown to the bus depot. It was still raining hard and blowing a gale. Between my luggage and my light-duty umbrella, it was quite a tussle getting across intersections, along streets and finally through the door of the Greyhound depot.

The first thing to strike my eye was a couple asleep in one another's arms, lying on the floor of the depot, against a wall. They were both very hefty, and lying together like that made me think of a small irregular mountain. Who are these people? I wondered. I sat down on a steel bench next to them, and awaited events. After a while they roused.

"Get a decent amount of sleep?" I asked.

"Ah… not too bad, really, thanks." the man said.

We chatted a bit. They were heading off on vacation to a place called Watertown, South Dakota, a spot I'd never heard of. I asked him what he did for a living.

"Oh, I produce safety videos for fire departments and search and rescue organizations."

This was not what I expected to hear. This huge man a minute before had been sound asleep on the bus station floor. I confess, I had clearly underestimated him. In my eyes, he'd been instantly transformed from an apparent *hobo,* into an intelligent, articulate producer of life-saving films. It's amazing whom you'll find sleeping on the floor in public places. We said goodbye, and he extended his hand to me, and I shook it. Another vignette from the road. It made me feel good.

I thought I'd break the bus trip into easy bits… not too long, and not arriving anywhere late at night. Accordingly, I decided to make my next stop Madison, Wisconsin, a city I knew nothing about except that it was placed conveniently between Minneapolis and Dubuque, Iowa. I was aiming for Dubuque because it is a major harbor on the Mississippi.

We rolled across the river into St. Paul. Although it is the state capital, and no doubt has many merits, I was eager to make some headway and so didn't bother investigating the place. One thing did catch my eye, however, on the eastern outskirts of the city. It was an enormous sign that said *3M*. Now this company has almost as much brand-recognition as Coca-Cola or McDonald's. I knew it is a successful, innovative multinational corporation, famous for... ah, let's see... Scotch Tape... Scotchguard... Post-It Notes... reflective fabric. In my mind, that was about it, apart from the fact that 3M is the new name of the Minnesota Mining and Manufacturing Company. I thought there must be much more to the company than that. So I checked it out; is there ever.

Not to bore you, but a few figures I came across indicate the importance of this firm. The company has patents on 55,000 products, employs 88,000 people and has annual sales of $30B. The variety of their products seems endless: adhesives, abrasives, laminates, dental and medical equipment, electronics, health-care items, traffic signals, to name a few. 3M has 132 factories world-wide and does business in 200 countries. They manufactured the last stethoscope I ever bought, the wonderful Littman Electronic; I loved it. I sold it to my own physician when I retired.

But honestly, Scotch Tape has to be my favorite 3M product. I've grown up with it, used it almost every day. We always have it in the house, and I know just where it is in the kitchen. We've tried cheaper brands, but they always tear, or shred, or break so you can't find the business end of the stuff. I'm a Scotch man for life. This is somewhat natural for me because it's rumored by our detractors that my family sprang from a line of sheep thieves in the Scottish lowlands.

I understand the tartan on Scotch Tape is that of the famed Wallace Clan. I wonder what William "Braveheart" Wallace would make of the whole thing. Doubtless he had weightier matters on his mind than household adhesives – matters that eventually got him hanged, drawn and quartered by King Edward I of England in 1305.

Scotch Tape was developed in the early 1930s as a way to seal the then-new product called *cellophane*. The original packaging bore the snappy slogan, *Seals Instantly Without Water.* How did the name Scotch come to be associated with it? Apparently someone was testing the prototype tape and noticed there wasn't enough adhesive on it to do the job. He's reported to have shouted, "Take this tape back to your Scotch bosses and tell them to put more adhesive on it!" The bosses, were not Scottish by nationality, but *Scotch,* a common insult of the day, meaning *stingy*. So that's where the name came from – and it has apparently stuck.

One more thing, before we leave this fond subject. For many years physicians have diagnosed pinworm (*Enterobius vermicularis*) infections in children by applying Scotch Tape – sticky side out – to a glass slide and using the sticky surfaces to pick up material around the patient's anus. The slide is then examined under magnification for the presence of the parasite... low-tech, but effective.

We rolled through gorgeous, prosperous farmland... all the corn in the world, handsome farms, shiny silos, smiling cows. About 75 miles into Wisconsin we arrived in Eau Claire, which is a beautiful and arresting name for a town, much more interesting than its English equivalent. It is, I later learned, the hometown of Mary Brunner, one of Charles Manson's myriad girlfriends; also Kato Kaelin, O.J. Simpson's onetime house-guest.

At the Eau Claire bus depot, two men in their forties got on; they took seats across the aisle from one another. They were jolly fellows, exchanging comments and jokes like old friends. After a few minutes of this, I figured out they'd actually just met. I thought maybe they were drifters, fugitives, ex-cons – birds of a feather, in a way.

They turned out to be birds of different feathers altogether.

The bigger one was Bruce, who sat one row behind me, in the

window seat. The first thing I noticed about him was that he had a complicated neck brace on, and from the livid scar on the front of his neck I could tell he'd had recent surgery. He bumped his head getting seated, and I blurted, "Oh, you poor bugger."

Our eyes met, and he smiled; we were away. He told us of how he was a trucker by trade, and had somehow rolled his semi, which he pronounced "sem-eye."

He found himself upside down with the roof of the cab crushing down upon the top of his head, kinking his neck severely. He had electric shocks running through his body. He was rescued promptly and had surgery soon thereafter. It was completely successful, and he was convalescing (likely without his surgeon's permission) by taking a bus ride to some town out west in order to pick up the car of his dreams – a '66 Camaro – and drive it back to Eau Claire. He talked about this car like a glutton talking about his next tenderloin; I believe I saw saliva on his lips.

Bruce was of Italian extraction, garrulous, wise and funny. He told us early on that he was an ex-Catholic, and there was something about him that reminded me of a priest I knew years ago: a roly-poly, philosophical, "winebibber and friend of publicans and sinners."

Bruce was indomitably cheerful. He says when anyone he's conversing with says anything gloomy, he says two cheerful things in return. Now, that might get mechanical and tiresome if it's overdone, but it's one way of steering a conversation into positive territory. My friend Ernie, in response to a depressing statement often replies, "But the good news is…," and then he'll say something like, "at least we're on the right side of the grass." In the world of today, how we do need aggressive optimists.

Somehow, the topic of our wives arose. Bruce told me he met his wife-to-be in a pawn shop, which I thought was rather novel. Both were married to others at the time, but curiously enough, they were both shopping for *rings*. A congenial conversation arose between them;

one thing led to many others, and now they're living – to hear him tell it – a life of great happiness. The state of their *exes* didn't arise... too gloomy to talk about, I guess.

Directly behind me sat Tony, a sandy-haired, clean-shaven man, with an open, honest face. I liked him instantly. Bit by bit he told me about his life, one of some *ups* and many self-inflicted *downs*.

After a few minutes of random talk, I asked him, "So what do you do?" This is a question that's part of normal conversation in some places (certainly the U.S.), and considered downright rude in others (especially England, in my experience). I really don't understand a person who is too timid or incurious to ask the question.

He told me his preferred line of work was as a drummer; usually with a certain top grunge-rock band in Wisconsin. He spoke wistfully of traveling in a van performing all over the Midwest. Somewhere along the line his luck ran out: his marriage collapsed, he was convicted of 'failure to support' his ten year-old son, and did jail time for offenses he was not prepared to specify.

At that point in his life, he was living in a storage compartment – with his drums – for $100 a month. Now that's thrifty living. Somehow he landed a job in Madison making pizza, a skill he had acquired somewhere along the way. I observed that it was a workday and asked why he was riding the Greyhound instead of working. He answered that the court required him to appear the day before in Eau Claire – something about child support, which, I was surprised to learn, is a *federal* offence.

Accordingly, authorities from Eau Claire picked Tony up in Madison two days earlier and took him back to Eau Claire for his judicial hearing. I had visions of two armed, uniformed law-enforcement officers arriving at Tony's storage locker, rapping on the steel door and handing him a subpoena. Poor Tony was cornered.

After the hearing, he was released on his own recognizance, with a state-funded bus ticket to Madison in hand. He worried that his uninsured truck might have been impounded while he was away; that would cost him $300. I reckoned he'd have to make quite a few pizzas for that.

In any case, he had obtained permission from his boss to be away from his job for the required duration, and he was planning to go back to work that very evening. Throughout, Tony spoke of his boss in such glowing terms I thought of the man as a complete *saint*. I'd love to have met him.

I really liked Tony. Looking back on his life of shambles, I imagine he must suffer from a degree of attention deficit disorder, based upon his evident challenges with family, work and finances. We stopped for a break at a roadside diner and I offered to buy him something to eat, but he refused, even though he looked hungry to me. It makes me sad to think of him.

His views on federal politics were thoughtful. He spoke well and precisely. I told him he had enough life experiences to write an interesting autobiography, and recommended Orwell's *Down and Out in Paris and London* as an example of what can be done creatively with hardship. He recommended *Galapagos* by Kurt Vonnegut, something to do with tourists breeding with Galapagos fauna. I'm pretty sure it wouldn't be my cup of tea. I was never a Vonnegut fan.

We eventually reached Madison, and I said goodbye to my companions. The quality of our conversation was excellent; I learned a lot from them, and was sorry to be leaving such good company. Before I left, I asked Tony to recommend a taxi company in Madison.

He said, "Give *Badger* a call. I used to work for them. They're good and real cheap."

I took his advice and phoned Badger. In a few minutes, a beater taxi came up with a driver who looked like he'd been driving a taxi for ten years too long. He was about 50, and was balding, but had a pony-tail. I noticed that his trunk was half-occupied by a natural gas tank. He was not too communicative, so, to get the ball rolling, I asked him if he was happy with the fuel economy.

"Indeed," he said, "*one* gets about 200 miles to the tank." Now it's not every day you hear that turn of phrase. Later, he disclosed he earned an M.A. in writing fiction from Johns Hopkins. I told him I had him pegged for a literary type because of the way he used the word *one*, when describing his mileage. We both laughed. I subsequently learned that several celebrities worked as cabbies at one time: Larry David, creator of *Seinfeld*; playwright David Mamet; actor Danny Glover and composer Philip Glass, to name a few. Driving a cab... I imagine it's a great way to learn about people, about life.

I had intended to spend just one night in Madison, but, as you'll see, this was not to be. The next morning as I was walking past a McDonald's, I saw a woman who looked about sixty sitting on the sidewalk, facing away from me. As I approached, I could see she had a big umbrella for shelter, and a battery-powered radio beside her. She sat on an orange beach towel. She had a sign on either end of her encampment. The one I could read said *I'm McStruggling – Can You Help?* Well, I thought that was pretty good, and it appealed to my better nature. I slipped her a gift; she said, "God bless you, sir." She'd have made an interesting Dickens character – an associate of *Oliver Twist,* perhaps. I'd liked to have interviewed her, but I decided that would be invading her privacy; I simply wished her well, and walked on. People like that arouse the 'rescuer' in me.

That got me thinking of homelessness, which is an enormous, seemingly insoluble civic problem wherever you go. Some call it houselessness; there must be much hopelessness to it, too.

There are parks in certain cities where it's illegal to lie down on a park bench. Some libraries forbid patrons to close their eyes; others, I understand, enforce a *dress code*, of all things. On a personal note, I remember spending a lovely afternoon dozing on a park bench by the

River Cam in Cambridge; mercifully, no constable told me to "move along."

Of course, there are several causes of homelessness. A major one is the huge number of uncared-for mentally ill patients. In the sixties, it was thought mentally ill patients would do better if released from 'institutions' and treated as out-patients. Accordingly, in 1967, Governor Ronald Reagan signed the *Lanterman-Petris-Short Act*, which resulted in the de-funding of hundreds of mental health treatment centers. This led to the virtual abandonment of untold numbers of these patients – to fend for themselves. Most were lost to follow-up; many ended up on the streets, unable to manage their own lives.

One U.S. study estimated that each homeless person costs the taxpayer $31,000 a year, mostly through law-enforcement and medical costs. Allow me to suggest a possible solution to the problem, as unfashionable as it may seem. I think the chronically homeless in a given city should be rounded up and cared for in a publicly-funded institution – what one might call a 'hospital trade school.' Each resident would be assessed in terms of needs and assets. The mentally ill, especially schizophrenic and bipolar patients, would be required to accept proper treatment. Addicted residents would be similarly required to accept treatment.

Moreover, those residents without job skills would be enrolled in training programs to prepare them for gainful employment. There would be a merit system whereby residents could graduate from the place if they've done well in their programs. First would come day-passes, which would be used to search for work. Once an appropriate job had been secured, the resident would qualify for probationary discharge. Obviously, all residents would not graduate from the place, but instead would be respectfully cared for, and given appropriate liberties. Such a plan is bound to raise a hue and cry from certain quarters, but the fact remains that what most cities are doing now is clearly not working. We simply can no longer tolerate large areas of our cities that are filled with homelessness, poverty, addiction and crime – areas where law enforcement fears to tread. The City of San Diego has a scheme similar to the above, which, I'm happy to see, is relatively successful.

Interestingly, Russia has a different way of dealing with housing. There, the 'right to shelter' is guaranteed by the constitution. Unused privately-owned real estate can be commandeered by the state and converted into public housing. Moreover, if a borrower is unable to pay his or her mortgage, the bank is compelled to find that customer cheaper accommodation. Can you beat that for financial fantasy – it's like making up a new type of mathematics – good luck with that! This plan strikes me as more heavy-handed than the one I proposed. No doubt the *FSB* – offspring of the KGB – facilitates this with their customary brutish methods.

As I walked around this part of Madison I noticed an astonishing number of *drive-thrus*. These things have rather taken me unawares. If they did not actually exist, they would be incredible to me. Who is so short of time they have to 'drive-thru' Starbucks, or In-N-Out Burger... seriously!

I don't think they're good for people; I'll bet drive-thrus lead to acid-reflux, hypertension, ulcers and a host of damaging physical and psychological phenomena.

I thought the drive-thru must be an American idea. It's all about speed, convenience, competition, busyness, shortage of time and scrambling from one thing to another – pretty much the North American *modus operandi*. Can you imagine the French or Italians relating to these things? Life in those countries is *arranged around* mealtimes – times of conviviality, pleasure, relaxation – features associated with a good, long and pleasant life. To buttress my case, I note the average life-expectancy in France is 82, in Italy, 83 and in the U.S., 79. The figures speak for themselves, and implicate as accomplice, I believe, the odious drive-thru.

Doing a little digging, I learned the drive-thru indeed originated in the U.S. The first drive-thru restaurant opened in 1947 – Red's Giant Hamburg, in Springfield, Missouri, located on Route 66. In the intervening years, several types of business have adopted the idea. We are now blessed with drive-thru banks, mailboxes, grocery stores, pharmacies, funeral homes and marriage chapels. Drive-thru liquor stores are jocularly known as *brew-thrus*. Every so often some non-conformist tries his luck at a drive-thru. Some pedestrians have tried to *walk-thru* a designated drive-thru. Bicyclists have tried it, as have folks in horse-drawn carriages and on ride-em lawnmowers. I even walked through a drive-thru myself once, just to see how they'd react. Nobody batted an eye.

I was at a bit of a loose end that day in Madison. I walked aimlessly through the streets around my hotel. All I could think of was getting onto the Greyhound to Dubuque on time. I reserved a Badger cab with plenty of time to spare; I had to get to a certain Arby's across town, which served as the bus depot. As I was waiting outside my hotel, a Brinks armored truck rolled up. The driver whisked into the hotel and his buddy stood squarely between the truck and the doorway. Our eyes met, and he bellowed, "How're ya doin'?"

I jumped, and blurted out, "Good! You?"

"Purdy good!"

Well, he was a big ol' friendly boy, with a broad smile; he had a gap between his two front teeth, like Ernest Borgnine. On one hip was an enormous pistol, on the other two long ammo clips. The smile and the gun made a crazy juxtaposition; it surely sent a mixed message. I started wondering about Brinks, which has been part of the cultural landscape as long as I can remember.

Brink's had a humble start. In 1859, one Perry Brink of Chicago bought a horse and wagon. He called this outfit Brink's City Express; its main work was transporting railroad passengers' luggage to their hotels. The business developed nicely; by 1872 Brink operated twenty wagons to all parts of Greater Chicago. Part of his success was that his fees were less than his competitors' – a quarter was all it cost to deliver a trunk anywhere in the area.

Sadly, Brink died of encephalitis at age 42, but his 19-year-old son, Arthur, took over. Arthur was a sharp lad, I gather, and together with three other investors expanded the company, incorporated and started selling shares. In the late 1800s, hard times hit the economy and Brink nimbly shifted his focus to transporting *money*. His first such shipment took place in 1891; it consisted of six sacks of silver dollars, totaling 366 pounds. It all sounds rather quaint, from our viewpoint. Brink's went from victory to victory and by the time the 1893 Chicago World's Fair rolled around, Brink's was the only game in town for money transport.

In 1904 the company bought its first motorized vehicle, a Knox Gasoline Express Wagon. Although some complained of fumes and noise – and the horses found it disturbing – Arthur commented that this new rig could do the work of three wagons and twelve horses.

The intervening history of Brink's is interesting enough, but we don't want to overdo the subject. Suffice it to note that today the company now has annual revenue of $4B, operates in a hundred countries, employs 70,000 people, and operates 7,800 trucks. Old Percy would be tickled.

Every so often you hear of a guard thumping his colleagues over the head and stealing the loot. This excites my interest no end – providing there's no bloodshed, and the loss is insured. However, my favorite account of a Brink's robbery is the *Great Boston Brink's Robbery* of 1950. This actually occurred at the Brink's Building in the north end of Boston. This was spearheaded by a small-time hood named Tony "Fats" Pinocchio and his gang of ten.

The gang trained for *two years* – copying keys, monkeying with locks, doing dry runs, and the like. On the evening of January 17, wearing Halloween masks and chauffeur's hats, they slickly entered the building and took close to $3M in cash and checks; this was the biggest heist in U.S. history up to that time, and was completely bloodless. Naturally, it was dubbed 'the crime of the century.' The public loves this stuff, and most people seem to root for the crooks. Why is that?

Sadly for Fats and the boys, by 1956 all were rounded up by the FBI; the court handed down life terms to everyone. Oddly enough, all were paroled in 1971; this, to me, suggests a pay-off. The most suspicious thing about the robbery is that only $58,000 was actually recovered by authorities. By astute deduction this cache was found hidden in a wall in a Baltimore office building. What happened to the rest of the loot is anybody's guess.

Meanwhile, back in Madison, I'd arrived at Arby's on the edge of town, where I was planning to grab my bus. I must have arrived an hour early, such is my compulsion for punctuality. I held my ticket in a death grip.

In front of the restaurant door a black couple was quarreling in the most unrestrained manner – like the sort of argument a couple might have in private – before someone gets killed. Honestly, I thought they'd come to blows.

I settled in for my hour's wait. Ten minutes went by, and I was surprised to see them, still outside, smoking amicably together; they must have declared a cease-fire. They came into the restaurant and ordered a huge serving of curly fries; they picked at them in a desultory manner – putting in time till their next smoke, I figured. I monitored their conversation as best I could; I reckon two-thirds of the words were profanity of the most dreary sort, which I'll leave to your imagination.

Well, eventually it was about 4:30, half an hour after my bus was to have arrived, and still no Greyhound. It dawned on me that something serious was amiss. I asked the lovebirds described above if they were waiting for the bus. The fellow snarled a reply in my direction, indicating they were not. I asked the same question of another young woman who appeared to be waiting. She said she was, and together we figured out that the bus we were supposed to have taken was not a *Greyhound,* but rather one of the *Lamer's* line – which pulled out half an hour earlier! I could feel my blood pressure shoot up, and my face suffusing. I was *lame,* indeed... more like dead in the water.

Here was my situation: I had good, but non-refundable, accommodation prepaid for that night in Dubuque. I had no reservation for that night – a Saturday – in Madison. The next bus wasn't for 24 hours. I needed a bed for the night. I started calculating the money this screw-up was going to cost me, and it only made me feel worse. I considered taking a taxi to the airport and flying to Dubuque.

Just then, however, I looked out the window and saw a motel across the street, a Day's Inn. This is a chain of hostelries of quite uneven quality; nevertheless, I gave them a call. I think the receptionist sensed my desperation. She said her name was Ramona, and she called me "Hon" a couple of times; I liked that. I told her my story, and she made sympathetic noises. In any case, she did have a room, but at a greatly inflated rate of $200; I heard her smile as she quoted the rate. Well, I thought: this place had better be good.

By this time it was raining and blowing, rather in keeping with the general tenor of the day; I had to make it across six lanes of traffic with my luggage and my umbrella. Curiously enough, I couldn't see how to get to the front door of the place, all was obscured... my glasses fogged up. I could see, however, a big water-filled ditch between me and my destination.

Well, I did the only thing that I could think of: I chucked my two pieces of baggage and my umbrella across the ditch, took a deep breath and made running jump. I landed a trifle awkwardly, twisting my right knee a bit. Never mind, I was across; I straightened myself up and strode, as debonairly as I could manage, into the hotel.

On the way through the door I met a lady with a Border Collie and I took time to make up to the dog, a breed I love. I was feeling better already; I could feel my blood pressure drop agreeably. Do I ever love dogs – it doesn't matter if they're small as rats or big as bears – except, of course, in the case of Dachshunds, to which I have a fixed aversion. Besides: they're ugly, ill-tempered, allergenic, and I can't stand 'em – weenies!

I hate the expression 'killing time,' especially at my age. In any case, I spent most of the next day loitering around the motel and jawing with the manager, Bernard. I get the impression that everyone here is mad about sports; Bernard sure was. He told me about the University of Wisconsin Badgers football team and how there was a 'big game' with a college from Alabama coming up that day. Now, college football doesn't exactly get my blood up, but he informed me that this team has been really outstanding since the early 1990s, winning three Rose Bowls and numerous Big Ten championships. I covered my ignorance by nodding sagely, and smiling. In a way, it was pleasant to hear his boyish enthusiasm. He reminded me of how people used to talk in the early sixties, e.g., "How 'bout those Badgers! Aren't they havin' a swell season? Should get the pennant, for sure!"

It was time to head back to the bus. I felt a lot more alert than I'd been the day before – maybe something to do with the $200 sleep. In any case, I planned to catch the proper bus that day at three. I walked over to the 'depot' which was a combined restaurant and a Phillips 66 gas station. The shared marquee showed the emblems of both companies. The message on it suggested folks should *Try Our Sliders*. It was unclear to me if these were menu items or lubricants. The word *sliders* reminds me of mucus or phlegm. No thanks.

There was no fooling me that day. I saw the Lamer's bus at the curb and I ran over waving my new ticket; I established that this was indeed the one to Dubuque. *Halleluia!* My relief was enormous, to think I'd be rolling again after being practically hamstrung for a couple of days. Well, the Lamer's bus was fine, and carried only six passengers. The driver was a very pleasant woman who greeted me enthusiastically. I noticed that she'd had a hare-lip scar. One can imagine the anguish of a young girl growing up with that sort of facial feature. In any case, she was sweet to all the passengers and I liked her instantly; moreover, she was an excellent and confident driver.

This bus was equipped with seatbelts, a real oddity in North America; they are mandatory elsewhere, say, in the U.K. I remember an accident that occurred in Yorkshire when a bus in which my wife and I were traveling hit a sports car at an intersection. It was quite a wallop, and I'm glad we had our belts on.

Honestly, what argument could you make against seatbelts in buses? Bus accidents are common, and characterized by gruesome death and dismemberment, a lot like a plane crash. In my part of the world they are usually tour buses full of foreign visitors. Whenever they do crash, it's a true disaster – which usually overwhelms emergency departments of all nearby hospitals.

Virtually all the studies concerning buses and seatbelts relate to school buses; they are statistically very safe. One report reassuringly states that only "a handful of children" are killed annually in school bus accidents – as if a handful of dead children wasn't much to worry about. Comparing the safety of a school bus creeping through city streets to a Greyhound hurtling down the Interstate, however, is simply nonsense. The 'no seat-belt' crowd reminds me of those creepy tobacco executives who denied knowledge of the dangers of smoking. Basically, those not in favor of seatbelts cite the added cost of equipping buses with them. Interestingly, the *driver* is legally required to wear one. Little by little, though, things are improving. Currently, six states require seatbelts in school buses, and 80% of all new buses are equipped with them. About time!

As we rolled along I was astonished at the immensity of the cornfields that ran off in every direction as far you could see – worlds of the stuff. Until that time, I'm sure I'd never spent more than a minute thinking about corn; I just took it for granted... nice but not very interesting. However, obviously folks in this part of the world are obsessed with it, and I thought I should get the gist of plant and its influence.

First, one must get it straight that the word *corn* is used differently in different countries. In most places it means *grain*, or a certain type of grain – in England *corn* means *wheat*, in Scotland and Ireland it means *oats*. What people call corn in North America is more properly called *maize*, or Indian corn; this is what I was seeing so much of through the window of the bus. Iowa and Illinois are called the *Corn Belt* for good reason – it's the best place in the *world* to grow it. I find the fact amazing.

Maize is indigenous to the Western Hemisphere. In 1492 – a very busy year indeed – Christopher Columbus discovered corn being cultivated on the island of Cuba. Studies indicate it came into being in Mexico and spread to suitable regions of the Western Hemisphere – all the way from sea level to the Andes. For the indigenous peoples – Aztecs, Mayas and Incas – the growing of corn was of paramount importance. One article I read stated, "Corn is perhaps the most thoroughly domesticated of all field crops. Its perpetuation has for centuries depended wholly on the care of man." Thus, the significance of corn is absolutely enormous; I'm shocked at my ignorance of the subject.

More than 40% of the world's maize is grown in the U.S. The main type is known as *dent* corn, because, logically enough, it has a *dimple* in the middle of each kernel, a little belly-button. Isn't that the darnedest thing? How many corn kernels have I eaten and never noticed that? Maybe they disappear when cooked; I'll have to check.

In the late nineteenth century, sixty million acres of corn were grown in the U.S. By 1917, it had increased to 111,000,000 acres, roughly the area of the state of California. The average yield per acre until the 1930s was about thirty bushels. Through improved management, this has steadily grown; in a recent year the Iowa acre yield had risen to a stunning 142 bushels. A bushel of ears of corn, incidentally, weighs 56 pounds.

Most corn production goes into feed for cattle, poultry and hogs. About 6% is made into high-fructose corn syrup (HFCS), the same percentage is fermented and refined into ethanol fuel. Corn mash is fermented and distilled into the whiskey known as *Bourbon*. It's not certain how Bourbon got its name – it depends on who's doing the talking – but some say that it comes Bourbon Street in New Orleans, where it was often served in place of the more expensive French *Cognac* to innocent patrons.

Before we pass on, a word about high-fructose corn syrup may be in order. In my experience, no one seems to have a good word to say about it; much opinion on the subject is poorly-informed. *Consumer Reports* in 2010 noted that the composition of HFCS and cane sugar are essentially the same: half fructose and half glucose, and are equivalent in calories. More recent studies failed to find any evidence that HFCS causes more health problems (obesity, diabetes, metabolic syndrome) than table sugar made from sugar cane or sugar beets.

So, just for fun I decided to think of all the words or terms I could with *corn* in them. Here goes: corny, corn flakes, corn-cob, Cornwall, authors Patricia, Bernard and John Cornwell, corn maze, cornicle, Corning, popcorn, cornstarch, Cornhuskers, cornmeal, corn-bread, cow-corn, corn-flower, corn-pone, unicorn, corn syrup, corn belt, corned beef, corn broom, corn dog, peppercorn, corn snow, foot corns, cornet, cornice, corner, cornball, corn-boil, corn whiskey, corn oil, cracked corn, acorn, cornea – in all, a veritable *corn*ucopia. Sorry, I couldn't resist.

Well, I'm happy to report I was delivered without fanfare to the absolutely splendid new bus depot in Dubuque, Iowa. I'd never been in Iowa before, knew little about it, but was eager to learn. My main reason for being there was that Dubuque is a major port on the Mississippi. I was the only person in the whole depot, which was a little eerie.

I grabbed a cab – a smart hybrid of the *Green* line – to the Motel 6 on Dodge Street, and booked in for two nights. I really like booking for more than one night. If you're shoving off after your *first* night, you can't really let your hair down; you can't relax, sleep in, have a lazy breakfast. You have to defend your room against 'housekeeping' arriving at 0730 hours, with brooms, vacuums, mops, dusters, sponges and other implements of cleanliness. Moreover, you must launch yourself into the cold world at 11:00, whether you feel prepared for it or not. It's all too abrupt, and gets my acid-reflux going.

If, on the other hand, one books for two nights, it's like a mini-vacation. One might almost unpack one's luggage into the chest of drawers most places provide. There's simply no comparison between a one- and a two-night stay.

The proprietress, whom I'll call Lena, was most obliging. She really could not have been more pleasant and communicative. She, her husband and her dog, Cinnamon, live on-site, a couple of doors down from my unit. The most remarkable thing about her was her voice, which she could scarcely raise into my audible range, a result of laryngeal cancer and its treatment. There was nothing, however, about her that suggested self-pity or embarrassment. She explained to me that she and her husband had been long-haul truckers for many years; they would switch-off driving every few hours, around the clock, traveling the Midwest and occasionally as far as California. She told me they used to "haul cheese for Kraft," which required them to drive their rig into a certain limestone cavern in Missouri for pick-up. I got great pleasure thinking of this couple working and traveling endlessly together; I'll bet they did it with keen interest, good cheer and a bit of free cheese here and there.

Well, my first day in Dubuque was Sunday. I had to get down to the river and I asked Lena about a city bus to the huge National Mississippi River Museum.

She said, "Buses don't run Sun-dy." I found this unexpected, refreshing and rather nostalgic.

"No problem," thinks I, "I'll walk." So, I set out.

A few paces along I saw a sign at a Dunkin' Donuts shop, which read, *Gets you going and keeps you going*. One wonders to which bodily function they are referring. Naturally, cars thronged the drive-thru. Ah, the wonders of caffeine and sugar – what mighty gifts to the human race! I'd love to see what would happen to society if deprived of these essentials for, say, a year.

Take coffee alone. It would be really ugly; folks convulsing in the street, others staggering around like zombies. A general lassitude would prevail; productivity would tank, businesses fail, GDP shrink, the economy collapse. The Great Recession would seem like a picnic by comparison. Worst of all, because coffee is the so-called *Think Drink*, people would actually stop thinking. God forbid.

I walked in the right direction along Dodge Street, but after five minutes I ran out of sidewalk, or even a safe place to walk. I hustled back to the motel and I told Lena the situation. She proceeded to give me a baffling set of directions on how to walk to the River. I nodded like I was paying attention, but in my mind I said, "Hey, I should have so much time!"

I discretely stepped outside and called Green Taxi. Dealing with this company, somehow I felt I was doing the environment a favor.

I'll resist giving you myriad facts about the Mississippi River, *The Father of Waters*; such are easily obtained elsewhere. What I'd like to do is relate my general impressions of it, noting features that struck me as unexpected or exciting.

I took a lovely, sunny, breezy stroll along the Dubuque riverfront and gleaned a few nuggets. I had no idea, for instance, that the River was included in the *Louisiana Purchase of 1803*. President Jefferson bought over 800,000 square miles of North America, then part of colonial France, from Napoleon Bonaparte – who needed to fund his military ventures. The cost (in 2014 dollars) was forty-two cents an acre, surely the most astute real estate deal in history.

In those early days, rivers were the 'highways' of the young nation; steamboat traffic appeared on the Mississippi in 1823. Early steamboat commerce was limited, however, because of the shallowness of the river in many places. As a result, a network of railroads developed to transport people and goods to a young and growing country. The railroad superseded the river in commercial importance for many years; the full commercial potential went unrealized until the 1930s.

I am absolutely amazed at human ingenuity under pressure – war, depression, catastrophe of all sorts. A great many interesting things happened in this country during – and because of – the Great Depression. An achievement of the first order occurred when the U.S. Army Corp of Engineers was commissioned to modify the Mississippi for commercial purposes. The aim was to turn the river into one of the great waterways of the world, while providing jobs in an otherwise depressed economy. The project was an absolute tonic to the nation. These chaps went to work dredging and rerouting the river, and constructing 29 locks and dams. Their work rendered the river navigable for much of its length, and actually altered some state boundaries, leaving a sliver of, for example, Illinois, on the west bank, whereas before the work, the entire state was on the east bank. Seasonal flood threats were much reduced by their work.

I was also amazed to learn of the lack of hydroelectric development along the river. There are, however, many such proposals at the moment; the time may be right. The good news is that many of the present dams can be quickly and cheaply modified to generate electricity, with low environmental impact. We do live in interesting times.

I dutifully toured the magnificent museum. It is surpassingly well done, but the overall effect on me went beyond sobering, to downright depressing. The designers of the National Museum of the Mississippi River assert, in effect, "We love, we venerate, the River, but evil *Man* through stupidity and greed has turned it into a giant sewer, full of the off-scouring of modern civilization. We should hang our heads in shame; we should panic; we should snuff ourselves out, at least five billion of us."

It reminds me of the *Confession* we recited when I was an Anglican: "We have left undone those things we ought to have done, and we have done those things we ought not to have done; And there is no health in us."

Well, I can tell you, I'm fed up with such environmental pessimism. We so focus on our environmental problems, we're apt to be paralyzed by discouragement. Most everybody's crying the environmental blues – millions of pessimists. There's even a organization, the Voluntary Human Extinction Movement, whose aim is to persuade people to refrain from reproducing, till the race peters out – all for the good of the 'biosphere.' There's a cheery perspective!

We can't afford such pessimism. Much work is required, of course, but as a society we're smart enough, rich enough and creative enough to do what needs to be done. Take the River Thames, for instance. Starting in the 14th century, London's sewage and refuse was dumped into the river. Fifty years ago it was declared "biologically dead"; fish were suffocated by the bacterial byproducts of the sewage.

Since the sixties, however, measures have been taken to 'clean up the Thames' mainly by modernizing the management of sewage, adding fish ladders and creating habitat for plants and wildlife. A volunteer program exists whereby interested groups can 'adopt a mile' of riverbank to keep tidy. The Thames Sewer Tunnel is scheduled for completion in 2020, after which the river will be 'exceptionally clean,' according to experts. Even today, dolphins have been seen well upstream in the Thames. That's what the Mississippi needs – optimism, intelligence and effort, not hand-wringing and misanthropy.

There were many illuminated quotations throughout the museum; everybody has something to say about the Mississippi. One I particularly like was by A.A. Milne; and who doesn't have a soft spot for that wonder-writer? "Sometimes, if you stand on the bottom rail of a bridge and lean over to watch the river slipping slowly away beneath you, you will suddenly know all there is to be known." To me, that's glorious, because it's somewhat, but not completely, comprehensible. In any case, I felt electrified when I read it, and I'm not quite sure why. I think it's because the idea works on an emotional, not intellectual, level.

Well, after the museum experience, I needed to clear my head so I bought a ticket on the paddlewheeler, the *Spirit of Dubuque*. Outside the ticket office was a sign that made me smile,

ALL GAMBLERS AND FANCY WOMEN
MUST SIGN UP WITH CAPTAIN
BEFORE BOAT LEAVES FOR NEW ORLEANS.

The trip was narrated by a very odd stick indeed. He sounded as though he was drowsy to the point of losing consciousness from time to time. I remember thinking that I hoped this guy wasn't at the helm. He would stop in the middle of a sentence, which made getting the gist of what he was saying rather challenging. At one point, he was talking about the Mount Carmel Convent which we could see up on the hillside, off the starboard bow.

"At one time," he said, " there were 1,000 nuns there. Now there are only five..." Several seconds passed. I was wondering how this quintet was making ends meet. Then he added, "hundred." The effect was comical, but a bit disorientating, and certainly affected my understanding of his narration.

Thus he delivered loads of information on the river, past and present. I was particularly intrigued by the convent. The Mount Carmel Convent is home to a Catholic community known as the Sisters of Charity of the Blessed Virgin Mary. In 1831 a group of five Catholic women led by Mary Frances Clarke came together to teach the poor children of Dublin. They soon were directed to Philadelphia to teach the children of Irish immigrants there. They became known the 'Sisters of Charity' in 1833. Ten years later, they went to Dubuque, mainly to address the issue of girls' education, which was sadly lacking at the time. Accordingly, the Sisters established a boarding school on the prairie near Dubuque. From this humble beginning evolved Clarke University, currently a thriving co-ed liberal arts college with a staff of six hundred, and a student body of twelve hundred. Good going, Sisters!

Mercifully, the narrator finished his script as the boat pulled into its berth. We passengers clapped, partly to be polite, but mostly to warm our hands, I figured. On the way back to the motel in the cab we passed the Hotel Julien Dubuque at Second and Main, which, I recalled from the boat narrative was once visited by Al Capone and his entourage; they filled the top three floors. Does that set the mind a-whirl, or what? Imagine, three floors-full of Chicago hoods in little old Dubuque. Did they use assumed names? Did they all 'pack heat'? What did they talk about? Did they get room service, or did they all barge into the dining room together without reservations? How did they behave with the staff? Did they ever go out bowling, or to a movie? Did they pay their bills, or did they sneer and set fire to them with big cigars? It occurred to me that old Scarface might have been holed up there with his *consigliere* and dozens of accountants working on his tax problems. (You will remember that Capone's legal downfall was due to income tax evasion.)

Now I've long been mesmerized by the Mob – admittedly an un-wholesome interest. So I'll resist the temptation to delve into details of the life of that devil Capone – such as the fact he was called *Snorky* by his friends because he was a sharply-dressed man. But while I was in Dubuque, I learned that Capone's lawyer was a shyster known as "Easy Eddie"; I just had to find out about someone with such a slick nickname. I'll bet he stayed with the gang at the Julien. I visualize him going down to the lobby to have his shoes shined every day by a black man named Nat. Eddie was probably a heavy-tipper.

Easy Eddie was, in fact, Edward J. O'Hare, born in 1893 in St. Louis, the son of Irish immigrants. By the time he was thirty he'd earned a law degree and joined a local law firm. Not long after graduation he developed an interest in the sport of dog-racing. He actually helped invent the mechanical rabbit that greyhounds chase; this gizmo made him a fortune.

Seeking more riches and excitement, he moved to Chicago in 1927, right in the middle of the Prohibition era. He soon met Capone, boss of the notorious Chicago Outfit and the city's most prominent citizen. The Outfit's activities includes racketeering, gun-running, bribery, bombing, arson, burglary, murder, money laundering, gambling and – most lucrative of all – *bootlegging*. This of course involved the illegal importation of spirits from Canada, where – most say wisely – Prohibition had been repealed.

Capone had a free hand in the city, with the implicit cooperation of the police and judiciary. O'Hare and Capone got along well at first, and engaged in much lucrative monkey-business. In spite of his seeming legal immunity, Capone figured a man with his type of business interests should retain a sharp lawyer; Easy Eddie amply filled the bill.

Capone, O'Hare and the Outfit continued to prosper for a few years, but criminal enterprises are inherently unstable and liable to draw attention from senior levels of law enforcement. The reasons are complex, but by 1930 O'Hare had decided to distance himself somewhat from the Outfit. Some say he had become ashamed of his lifestyle, especially in the eyes of his son, whose admiration he craved. Federal law enforcement was fully aware of Capone's activities, and was attempting to nail him; O'Hare must have gotten wind of this.

Accordingly, he approached reporter John Rogers of the *St. Louis Post-Dispatch* newspaper and asked him to arrange a meeting with the IRS, in order to spill the beans on Capone. O'Hare played a key role in Capone's subsequent prosecution and conviction. The IRS agent in charge was Frank J. Wilson, who, incidentally, eventually became Chief of the U.S. Secret Service. Years later, Wilson commented, "On the inside of the gang I had one of the best undercover men I have ever known: Eddie O'Hare."

In 1931 Capone was tried on tax evasion charges. Before the trial actually started, O'Hare tipped the government that Capone had fixed the jury. I'll bet everybody was ready for that old trick; Judge James Wilkerson nimbly switched juries with another federal trial running at the same time. Capone, then aged 33, was convicted and sentenced to eleven years, to be served mostly in Alcatraz. This strikes me as just the place for him.

By 1939, Capone had developed tertiary syphilis – little wonder – which qualified him for early parole. One week before the planned release, Easy Eddie was shot to death in his car by a group believed to be Capone confederates. Interestingly, this murder was never solved; one wonders how much effort the Chicago cops put into that one. At least Easy Eddie died with, one supposes, a clear conscience and a sense of redemption. In his pocket was found this note:

> *The clock of life is wound but once, and no man has
> the power to tell just when the hands will stop, at late
> or early hour. Now is the only time you own. Live,
> love, toil with a will. Place no faith in time. For the
> clock may soon be still.*

What for me seems the most amazing and unlikely facet of O'Hare's life concerns his son, Edward Jr., known as "Butch." This young fellow flew with the U.S Navy and displayed great bravery and effectiveness as a fighter pilot. In 1943, he died in action in the Pacific at the age of 29.

He received the Medal of Honor, the Navy Cross, two Distinguished Flying Crosses and a Purple Heart. One more thing: one of the busiest airports in the world is Chicago's *O'Hare International*. It's named in honor of Butch, but to be fair, I think Eddie Sr. deserves a little of the credit.

Well, by my second morning, I was eager to push off. I liked Dubuque, though – it's a civilized place, a *kind* place, based on my own limited experience. But I needed to get downriver, and no fooling about it. I reckoned I'd overnight in Davenport, one of the 'Quad Cities.' I'd never heard of this group of cities; they are Davenport and Bettendorf in Iowa and Rock Island and Moline in Illinois.

Knowing this didn't mean much to me, I must say. I needed to book accommodation so I selected a place in Davenport, and did some research on *Tripadvisor.com.* I found a well-priced place in Davenport; then I read a few reviews. One of them said the place looked pretty good from a distance, but the writer noted she found a quantity of *ashes* between the sheets (I'm guessing *cigarette*, but who knows?) I decided to give that place a big miss. I did, however, find a place in Bettendorf, namely the Isle Casino Hotel. I believe I've never even met *anyone* who's been to Bettendorf, so the sheer perversity of staying in a Casino Hotel there appealed to me. So I booked it.

As I was leaving the room, I heard a report on PBS radio direct from Townsville, Queensland, Australia telling us that it's so hot there that pythons are slithering into people's toilets to cool off. The announcer said with what sounded like a straight face that area residents were advised to turn on the bathroom light before doing their business. Aussies are a tough lot.

For the fourth time I called Green Taxi; off to the bus depot we sped. The driver was a pleasant lad of about forty. He wore snappy aviator shades. He was severely groomed: his face was freshly shaved, and although he looked bald, I could see that his scalp was completely covered with an extremely short stubble. His Oxford-cloth shirt was starched and pressed.

"If I had as much hair as you do," I said, "I wouldn't keep it so short."

He laughed. "I'm ex-Army, and my wife likes it like that. She shaves it once a week. Saves us a pile of money."

I guess you don't need a professional barber to shave your head. I imagined he'd be investing the savings for his son to go to West Point – maybe become a General. I was starting to like this fellow… clean, cheerful… a whistle-while-you-work kind of guy.

"I served in the infantry in Iraq in '03." Then he added cryptically, "I thought my dad might bomb me."

"What do you mean?" I asked.

"Well, my dad was in the Air Force," he said, "and he was real mad at me for goin' into the Army."

I furrowed my brow at that one. He was speaking metaphorically, because his dad was in one war, and he was in another, ten years later.

A few moments later I thanked him for his willingness to converse. "It seems to me," I said, "that cabbies who don't talk to their customers either don't like people, or they don't like their jobs, maybe both."

"Yeah, drivers like that are in the wrong job, for sure."

With effusive best wishes, we parted at the depot.

A few minutes later, I was standing at the front door of my bus; others milled around, sizing one another up, it seemed to me. A fellow traveler, a woman of about 45 looked at me and said, "Where *you* goin'?" She acted as though I had neglected to get her permission.

"Quad cities, probably Davenport." It had slipped my mind I had bookings in Bettendorf.

"Oh, my Gawd!" she exclaimed. "You don't want to go there! Way too dangerous… more shootings there than anywhere!"

In describing this woman, *babe* or *broad* would be about right. She was over-the-hill, forty pounds overweight, and possessed of the most unflattering fly-away platinum blonde hair I've seen for years. However, she was pleasant, tough, friendly and direct; I liked her style. How she ever got into her chartreuse bodice, I can't think; she'd have needed help.

Well, after she'd warned me about Davenport, she got onto her phone. I'm getting pretty good at listening to one half of a phone conversation, and inferring what the other person is saying. It was clear from what I – and many others – overheard was that she'd just been dumped by her boyfriend; she had no money and no place to stay. It hit me that one short phone call can make you homeless.

She needed help loading her bags into the luggage compartment. They consisted of one huge cardboard box and a dreadful, leaden, camouflage-pattern duffel bag. At the last second she decided to stuff some extra impedimenta (pillow, stuffed animals, hair-dryer, lamp) into the already-stuffed duffel. She straddled the bag, while I did up the flimsy zipper; it was quite an operation.

Just as she was about to board, she shouted to the driver, "I can't go!"

I confess, I was disappointed, because I rather liked this disorderly woman; she reminded me of a kind-hearted madam in a bordello. I thought of her as *Molly*. When I heard her say she couldn't go, I remember thinking she'll have to get her bags off the bus. Then what on earth will she do?

I needn't have worried. A few minutes after we got rolling I thought I heard her voice a few rows back. Sure enough, there was Molly, laughing and talking to her seat-mate like she hadn't a care in the world. How she got on without my seeing is a mystery; still, I'm glad she did. If you're homeless and broke, it's better to be rolling .

On this particular run, the bus company – Burlington Trailways – decided they'd inflict compulsory video entertainment upon their passengers by way of two tiny overhead screens. You could hardly distinguish the figures moving. These micro-screens were compensated for by an audio system that would pulverize granite. Honestly – I thought I'd go mad.

The show was the latest *Mission Impossible* which I'd seen before, and liked, but this was insufferable. At the first opportunity I asked the driver to tone it down. He said, "Sure, I can turn it off if you want."

"I don't want to spoil it for anyone who's watching."

"OK, then, buddy, how about I crank it back from nine to six?"

I agreed; I think everybody was happy with that.

In Waterloo a man boarded and took a seat one row ahead of me, across the aisle. He was a strange-looking, lumbering chap about sixty who looked like one of the villains in the *Mad Max* movies. The most striking thing about him was a large tattoo on his forehead – smack in the middle. His brow was wrinkled, so I couldn't tell what it represented; it looked to me like a crest of some sort, perhaps a coat-of-arms. I wanted to speak to him, but held off. After a while I figured I'd better plunge in.

"Excuse me, do you live around here?" I asked.

"Yes, I do… just up ahead, in Cedar Falls," he answered politely. The conversation rather lapsed at that point. I couldn't figure out how to get around to asking him about his tattoo. I'd left it too late.

A moment later, he asked, "Do you have a phone I could use for a moment?"

"Sure," I said, and passed it over.

"I've got to call my dad for a ride… he's only got one eye." The thought of a one-eyed octogenarian driving to the depot to pick up his son with the career-limiting facial tattoo struck me as rather poignant. Indeed, I felt sad for them both; but at least they had one another. I'd love to have heard their conversation.

About four we rolled into Davenport – *murder city*, according to my charming companion of earlier in the day. The city motto is *Working together to serve you*. More like *Working together to shoot you*, if what Molly told me was true. The city is also called 'Iowa's front porch.' Sounds just right for drive-by shootings.

Contrary to my expectations, I learned that Davenport's crime rate is actually falling, unemployment is low, real estate is affordable, and in a recent year it won the *City Livability Award* in the small-city category from the U.S. Conference of Mayors. Molly, poor dear, was operating on outdated information. Still, I was going to keep my eyes peeled.

Among a host of honorable distinctions, Davenport is home to Palmer College of Chiropractic, the first such school in the world, founded in 1897. Who doesn't have views on this field of endeavor?

My view is that they should change the name of their profession from *chiropractic,* which sounds like an adjective (e.g., traumatic, titanic, automatic, acoustic) to *chiropraxis*, which sounds like a noun to the sensible ear. Just think if we spoke of John Hopkins School of *Medical.* You do see what I mean.

Unfortunately, I was unable to find *chiropraxis* in any dictionary I consulted, including the one for *Scrabble*, but new words arise all the time, so I live in hope. This year's additions include zingers like *studerite, conceptor* and *tellinid.* In any case, the present name of Palmer College of Chiropractic is slightly slicker than the original one, *the Palmer School and Cure.*

Many physicians have held a jaundiced view of the principles and practice of chiropractic, claiming their methods lack scientific orientation and rigor. On the other hand, I know legions of regular folks that have greatly profited from chiropractic treatments, myself included. I'll let others argue with success, if they wish. One successful and ethical chiropractor I know says, "Science hasn't caught up with us yet."

I caught a cab and we headed north along the river to the adjacent city of Bettendorf, where, you'll remember, I'd arranged a room at the Isle Casino and Hotel. I'm impressed with how far your accommodation dollar goes when you stay at a hotel with a casino attached. It's assumed, of course, that the hotel guest will do some gaming during his stay.

What these hotel-casino owners may not know, is that I haven't spent a nickel in a casino for thirty years, so I'm certain these joints don't make any money off me at all. It's great – you can stay at a four-star hotel for *peanuts*, and the management doesn't ban you if you don't gamble – like they do if they know you're a blackjack card-counter. On my bedside table was a note pad with *Play More! Be Happy!* printed at the top of each sheet. Because the odds favor the house, I'd say the more you *play*, the happier management becomes. *Play more, make us happy*, however, doesn't sound quite as tempting.

Bettendorf is right on the Mississippi, which is one of its few assets, if I can believe my senses. I walked along the main drag, State Street, and a more dispiriting prospect would be hard to come by. The place just felt used-up and abandoned, a feeling only accentuated by the few pathetic businesses that were still sputtering along, and some tattered flags that welcomed one and all to 'Downtown Bettendorf.'

One of the truly remarkable things about Bettendorf was the rich assortment of goofy signs and business names, a real treasure trove in such an otherwise bleak spot. First up is the *Purgatory Pub,* featuring 'Eternal Fun and Sinful Food.' I had visions of a hapless tourist entering the place, then hearing a loud click as the door was bolted behind him. He'd stay there forever... to be tormented by hags with withered breasts – a kind of a nightmare Hooter's – supervised by a manager who had been expelled from the Faculty of Theology at Clarke University. How depressing can you get?

Up next was a joint called the *Scrub Pub.* Now this is really a clever idea. The premise is that you bring your dirty laundry in and put it into one of their coin-op washers. Then, instead of leafing through old copies of *People* or *Cosmo*, you take a seat at the bar and order a beer, maybe two. In due course, it's time for the dryer; an opportunity for another beer or two. In about an hour you're ready to head for home. Off you go with your clean laundry humming, *"Show Me the Way to Go Home."* This strikes me as a very pleasant way to get the wash done.

And then there was *Ed's Reconditioned Appliances,* upstairs from *Action TV Repair.* A more woebegone storefront can hardly be imagined. The signs were hand-lettered – perhaps by a child. The whole place looked as if it had been peppered with buckshot. I doubt they've repaired a TV there in the last 40 years.

Fumbles Sports Bar was located up a narrow staircase next to *Ed's.* I'd love to have gone in and met a few of the regular fumblers, but the place was locked up tight.

Along the way, so help me, was *Gravity Fitness Center.* Who came up with that crazy name? It sounds like the sort of place you'd exercise, and come out heavier than when you went in. It sucked the energy out of me just to read the sign. The experience might be like entering a *black hole,* or exercising on a planet with extra gravity, say, Jupiter.

My taxi driver next morning was the same one I'd had yesterday, a man named David. We rolled past Arsenal Island, off to the left, right in the middle of the river. David said there's a large Civil War cemetery there. I'm ashamed of my sketchy knowledge of the Civil War; I asked him what side Iowa fought on. What he replied shocked me; he said, "Many families sent half their sons to fight for the Confederacy, and the other half to fight for the Union."

As a father myself, what he said quite moved me; can you imagine what anguish and ambivalence such a family would have suffered? What a horrid way to hedge one's bets.

Arsenal Island is a fascinating place. For starters, at 2.6 square miles, it's the biggest island in the Mississippi River; it was originally called Rock Island. The Army has been active here since the early 1800s; an *arsenal* – a facility for the manufacture and management of armaments – was constructed here in 1862. During the Civil War, Confederate fighters – about 12,000 of them – were imprisoned here. Interestingly, many of the guards were from the 108th Regiment of *United States Colored Troops.* This must have really riled their Confederate prisoners and must have seemed cruel punishment, indeed. Sounds like poetic justice to me.

Here also is the Rock Island National Cemetery, established in

1863. Union soldiers – some 24,000 of them – were buried here by the war's end. Nearby is a separate cemetery for Confederate soldiers, 2,000 of whom died here in captivity.

In a way, I'd like to have visited Arsenal Island. I find military cemeteries enormously poignant – so much so I can hardly stand visiting such places. A military cemetery seems a terribly sad comment on human nature, and how poor we are at settling our differences in a civilized way.

This is one crowded island. I was astonished to learn that it's also the site of the largest government-owned weapons factory in the country. About 250 military personnel work here and 6,000 civilians. It's the U.S. Army's only foundry; it manufactures howitzers, small arms, aircraft weapons systems, grenade launchers and associated engines of war.

David dropped me at the depot. I looked around to see what was taking place; as long as there are other people to observe, there's always something of interest – overt or subtle – going on. What should I see... but a couple dressed in distinctive, sectarian garb. I asked myself, are they Mennonites, Hutterites, Anabaptists, Doukhobors, or what? I didn't think they were Amish, because they were traveling by bus. Naturally, I had to find out.

The husband wore a beard but no mustache. I stepped up to him and asked as politely as I could to what religious group he and his wife belonged. He turned to me with a neutral facial expression and said simply, "We're Amish."

I asked them if they were from Pennsylvania.

"No," he said, "we're from Canada... Aylmer, Ontario."

"Ah," said I cheerily, "the *Tomato Capital of Canada.*" I was sure of my ground.

"No, sir, that's Leamington," he replied.

So much for my confidence; I felt like I'd made a bad guess in *Trivial Pursuit.* I thanked him for straightening me out.

"Say, I thought the Amish didn't use mechanized transport," I said as benignly as I could.

"Well, we do use buses. But we don't own personal cars or trucks."

I thanked him again for enlightening me; that concluded our conversation. He was prepared to answer my questions, but was not what you'd call *engaging*. His wife was mute the whole time and largely concealed her face under her broad-brimmed bonnet.

Naturally, I pursued the Amish topic later, at my leisure. These are an interesting people – an ethno-religious group founded by Jakob Ammann in Switzerland in 1693. Ammann and his followers found their original sect, the Mennonites, too liberal and decided to leave the fold. In the 1700s they found their way to Indiana, Ohio, and Pennsylvania, and subsequently to many other states and, of course, as I'd just learned, to Ontario.

The main group are called *Old Order Amish*, and number 300,000, more than I'd ever have imagined. They have a veneration for the Bible, and live according to their understanding of its precepts. They engage in farming, most famously in Lancaster County, Pennsylvania; they esteem manual labor and humility; they eschew cars, trucks, tractors, electricity and telephones, and – I feel sure – the Internet.

They are monogamous and marry within their own communities. They don't usually practice contraception; the average couple has seven or so kids. They willingly pay their taxes, but do not wish to integrate with society at large, or accept Social Security benefits or participate in military activity. Because of considerable inbreeding, certain genetic disorders – for example, dwarfism – are relatively common among the Amish. On the other hand, they are remarkably resistant to skin cancer – which is a blessing to farming families.

The most remarkable event I know involving the Amish occurred in October, 2006.

This was the day one Charles Carl Roberts IV, a non-Amish milk-truck driver, entered the tiny schoolhouse in West Nickel Mines,

Lancaster County and methodically shot ten young girls, killing five of them. He then shot himself dead.

The facts of the case are easily obtained elsewhere, but the utterly glorious thing – the *miraculous thing* – about this ghastly event was how the community didn't give way to rage and despair, but instead sincerely *forgave* the murderer. Their elders advised community members not to even *think* evil of Roberts. One bereaved father said, "He has a mother and a wife and a soul and now he is standing before a just God."

Thirty members of the Amish community attended Roberts' funeral, and his widow was invited to the funeral of one of the little girls. What can one say in the face of such dignity?

After the interlude with the Amish couple it was time to board the bus for my next port of call, Hannibal, Missouri. I was unsure which syllable to emphasize; was it HANN-ibal, or Hanni-BAL? I didn't want to come across like a greenhorn, so I asked a thin, worn redhead in a black T-shirt and jeans standing nearby. She smiled at my ignorance, and said, "Why, honey, it rhymes with *cannibal.*" This is fact is worth knowing, especially if it's your destination, but the way she smiled when she said it gave me the shivers.

There were only five of us the bus for the first leg from Davenport to Burlington and I kept to myself, mostly reading *The Economist* and wondering what Hannibal was going to be like. At one point I ran across a quote of Garrison Keillor, whom I mentioned briefly above. "GK" is one of my favorites. As a raconteur, humorist, philosopher and writer he is superb. I'd call him America's preeminent philosopher of nostalgia. Speaking of travel, Keillor notes:

> *Travel is an art form available to Everyman. You sit in a coffee shop in some strange city, and no one knows who you are, or cares. So you shed your checkered past and your motley credentials, and you face the day unarmed... And onward we go, and some day in*

the distant future we'll turn around in astonishment to
see all the places we've been and the heroes we were.

All those who travel alone will have an understanding of what he's getting at. Solo travel is categorically different than traveling with a companion. Each day is very much more an adventure and challenge when you're on your own. Decision-making is straightforward – free from tedious negotiation – if not from blunders. In all the journeys described in this book, I don't believe I ever saw anyone else traveling alone, just for interest's sake. Traveling by bus is typically something one is forced to do by economic necessity – something to be endured rather than celebrated.

As we roll toward Hannibal, I'd like to consider the topic of *nostalgia* a little. Nostalgia is a huge issue for my generation. We 'boomers' wax on wistfully about how *good,* how *right,* how *wholesome,* everything was in the fifties, sixties and early seventies… our "good old days." We de-emphasize – or forget altogether – the many perilous difficulties of the time. Life in those days was just a bowl of cherries, to hear us tell it.

Nostalgia has been defined as "a sentimentality for the past, typically for a period or place with happy personal associations." It's from two Greek words conveying an *ache* for *homecoming*, a sort of homesickness for the past. It was first used in the 17th century in describing the emotional state of Swiss mercenaries far from home. If they'd stayed home making clocks, maybe the word would never have arisen.

Nostalgia is very big business; certain companies and communities make concerted efforts to stimulate – and then squeeze all they can out of this sentiment. We old-timers are happy to pay big bucks for the revival of our happy memories. It gets us right where we're weakest. A case in point is old U.S. Route 66, an unbroken nostalgia trip from 'Chicago to L.A.' If you ever want to experience full-on commercial nostalgia, that's your route. The kicks continue.

I changed buses in Burlington; the bus I boarded had only a

handful of passengers. I looked around to see who was aboard, any-thing to catch my eye. I'm fascinated by what people have printed on their clothing. They're sending the world messages: *Life's A Beach*, for instance, or *I'd Rather Be in Maui*, or *Aerosmith Global Warming Tour* – you know what I mean. The funniest ones are Japanese-made shirts with English words on them: *Precise Dwarf Bravery,* say, or *Expose Chicanery*, or *Crap Your Hands.* I'll bet people with messages on their shirts are also big fans of bumper stickers and not much given to critical thought.

Most clothing-slogans appear on T-shirts, with baseball caps com-ing in second. A few seats in front of me was a black chap with a cap with *Seabees* written on the back of the strap. Well, well, well, I thought, this fellow looks interesting. I had heard of Seabees since I was a kid and thought they were a tremendous bunch who undertook important military construction projects considered virtually impos-sible. I thought they'd been disbanded years ago, so I was curious about this solitary traveler and his new-looking hat.

The thing that stuck in my mind since I was a kid was the Seabees' motto, something to the effect they do *difficult* things immediately and *impossible* things take slightly longer. In fact, that is not the Seabees motto at all, but rather that of the U.S. Army Ordnance Department. The Seabees' official motto is *Construimus, Batuimus*, meaning *We build, We fight.* Their unofficial motto is simply *Can Do.* I just love that attitude.

I moved up and took a seat across the aisle from him. I asked him about his hat. To be honest, I was expecting him to say he got it at a thrift store. Before answering, he smiled, looked me in the eye, put out his hand, and said, "Hi, I'm Mike – I'm a Seabee vet."

What followed was one of the most interesting monologs I've ever heard. You couldn't really call it a conversation. I'd ask him a question and then he'd talk for about fifteen minutes until he had to come up for air – at which point I interjected a comment, or another question. Not once in three hours did he ask me a question.

I'll paraphrase our talk. He was a native of Brooklyn and was there on September 11, 2001. To my utter astonishment, he was a eyewitness to the collapse of the Twin Towers. It took me a moment to absorb what he was saying. Moreover, his brother was then a member of the New York Fire Department and was involved in their magnificent work that day.

Mike in those days had his own successful construction company. He was totally overwhelmed by what he'd seen, and this tragedy galvanized him into taking action. Two days later, with the support of his young wife, he went to a Naval recruiting center and signed up. When the Navy learned of his credentials as a builder, they assigned him to the Seabees.

By 2003 he had been deployed to Iraq with the job of rebuilding schools and hospitals damaged in the recent invasion. He was feeling secure and useful in his position, although he sorely missed his young wife. One afternoon he was working with a group of other Seabees on the flat roof of a hospital. Their rifles were stacked, tipi-style in the middle of the roof. The building site was being circled by several Humvees full of soldiers. All was proceeding according to plan, when suddenly they were interrupted by a mighty explosion in the center of the work site. Mike was blasted toward a concrete wall, head first. He lost consciousness.

"You can feel where my skull got cracked," he said to me. He encouraged me to feel his forehead. Sure enough; I could feel a linear vertical defect beneath the skin. He learned he had been the victim of an insurgent's rocket-propelled grenade. Mike was speedily evacuated to Ramstein Air Force Base in Germany for medical care, but his brain injury was serious and permanent. After a few weeks it was concluded he couldn't return to active service. He was awarded the Purple Heart, and promptly discharged home.

His wife was waiting for him. Mike casually mentioned that this woman was originally from Haiti – from a prosperous family, friends of the infamous Duvalier clan. He told me her father was a member of the Haitian Secret Police, the devilish *Tonton Macoute*. Mike said his father-in-law and his cohorts would pay night-time visits to certain citizens known for their non-support of the Duvalier regime, and simply shoot them in their homes. Many others were stoned, or burned alive. This era was characterized by unrestrained state terrorism; some 60,000 people are believed to have been murdered in this way. I worked in Haiti for a while and can attest to the people's utter terror of the *Macoute*.

In any case, Mike's wife was happy to see him, but somehow let it slip that she'd been lonely and had, on one or more occasions, been unfaithful to him. This shocked him terribly. In his way of thinking, the damage was done and there was no hope of reconciliation. His mental faculties were such that he was not able to think creatively about the problem; all he could think of was to get out – so he did. In those years, he'd lost everything: wife, home, ability to support himself, self-respect, the works. Again I was impressed how someone can become homeless in the twinkling of an eye, as the result of a single event.

In any case, he had been homeless for some years; he had worked intermittently, but never was able to reestablish himself. You'd never know it to look at him, though, or speak to him; he was well-dressed, well-spoken, well-groomed. He also seemed perfectly sensible, apart from the fact he talked incessantly. I wondered how he would have spent his time on the bus if I hadn't approached him.

He said he'd been diagnosed with Post-Traumatic Stress Disorder, so I presume he's on a pension. *PTSD* is much on our minds these days; most families seem to have been affected by it. I won't go into much detail here, but suffice it to say, it is an anxiety disorder that develops after a traumatic event – combat, sexual assault, natural disaster, traffic accident, terrorism and so on. Symptoms include flashbacks, memory disturbance, fearfulness, depression, anger, emotional detachment and drug abuse. The term was coined in the late 1970s when a 'stress-induced mental disorder' was noted in returning Viet Nam veterans. A similar syndrome had been observed in military personnel for at least 200 years, and has been variously known as *shell shock*, *soldier's heart* or *battle fatigue*.

I believe Mike's emotional state was compounded by a *traumatic brain injury* (TBI) involving his frontal lobes. In someone who's had his forehead collide with a concrete wall you might expect to find difficulties with impulse control, decision-making and planning. If you are trying to deal with both PTSD and frontal lobe injury, you can imagine the struggle that everyday life would be.

So, where, you might be wondering, was Mike going on the bus? Well, I was delighted to learn that his brother, a builder in Florida, had offered him a construction job beginning the next week, at a starting wage of $15 an hour. Mike was feeling good about making a new start, and wanted to "do it right this time." My time with this fine man was drawing to a close. It was a great blessing for me to have shared a little of his life. I felt impelled to encourage him to find a strong church in Florida, and I told him I'd pray for him. So long, Mike.... Godspeed, my friend.

Late that afternoon the bus rolled into Hannibal, Missouri. I'd chosen this place to visit for two reasons – the main one was the fact that it was the childhood home of Mark Twain. The other was that the Mississippi there is stunning to behold – broad and magnificent – and much involved with the history and spirit of the place. Some call Hannibal *America's Home Town*. No bus depot exists in Hannibal; this is a great shame. The bus stops at an unglamorous spot – Hardee's ("across from the KFC") out on Highway 61 – on the west side of town.

Now U.S. Route 61 is one of America's famous roads, known as the *Blues Highway*. Built in 1926, it's over 1400 miles long and stretches from the city of Wyoming in northern Minnesota to New

Orleans. Because it basically follows the Mississippi, it's also known as *The River Road.* It was by way of Bob Dylan's 1965 album *Highway 61 Revisited* that I first heard of it. On the eponymous first track of the album – the lyrics of which are clever-sounding gibberish to me – appears this verse:

> *Oh God said to Abraham, "Kill me a son"*
> *Abe says, "Man, you must be puttin' me on"*
> *God say, "No." Abe say, "What?"*
> *God say, "You can do what you want Abe, but*
> *The next time you see me you better run"*
> *Well Abe says, "Where do you want this killin' done?"*
> *God says, "Out on Highway 61."*

I'd decided to spend two or three days here and really dig into the place. Naturally, my first task was to get to my hotel, so I called the only cab company in town, a down-home outfit called Huck's Taxi Service.

A gruff voice answered with a single word: "Huck's."

I told this gent where I was and where I wanted to go. I was aware that my accent gave me away; he probably thought, "Who's this fancy-boy? I'll bet he's a limey!"

In a few minutes a battered purple Chrysler minivan arrived. On its roof was a cracked, faded light indicating it was indeed one of Huck's fleet – a fleet, I suspect, totalling *one.* The driver reminded me of a big sack of potatoes, heavy and shapeless; the driver's seat was splayed and crushed. I did my best to engage him in conversation, but evidently he wasn't in the mood, or maybe my accent put him off. Maybe he thought I was a Yankee. I don't know – maybe he had a toothache. In any case, it was a long quiet drive to my hotel on the river. I was bracing myself for a big fare.

"That'll be $3.75," he announced bluntly.

Well, I was so surprised at the modest fare that I handed him a five.

"Keep the change," I said, trying not to sound too grand.

"Thanks, Bud!" He seemed surprised by my largesse.

I lost no time taking a look around town. It was instantly obvious that this was "Mark Twain City." Everyone crowded onto the Mark Twain bandwagon... Mark Twain this, Mark Twain that. The Mark Twain Dinette was across from my hotel. The Mark Twain Lighthouse was just up the hill above the Visitors' Center. The Mark Twain Childhood Home was a few steps away, as was the Mark Twain Museum. The Mark Twain Hotel was just down the street. The Mark Twain Riverboat Experience beckoned at the river's edge. The Mark Twain Cave was just outside town. And if you need it, you can top up your respirator tank at Mark Twain Oxygen, out on the Interstate.

I climbed the 200 stairs to look at the Mark Twain Memorial Lighthouse standing on Cardiff Hill overlooking the city and the river. I adore and admire lighthouses, but this was more a gimmick than a real lighthouse, because it's not a navigational beacon at all, but rather a lightweight memorial to a local worthy. My view, as you will see, is that Twain's writing emitted as much *darkness* as it did light, so the lighthouse idea didn't really work for me. This appears to be the downside of writing satire.

But I was there, so I took a good look at it. It was originally built in 1934 and its light first shone forth when President Franklyn Roosevelt turned a 'golden key' in Washington, which everyone must have thought very sophisticated. It blew over (some lighthouse!) in 1960 and, after its re-erection was dedicated by President Kennedy. In the early nineties it was rebuilt and dedicated once again, this time by President Clinton.

I spent the evening walking as many streets of the town as I could, fanning out from downtown. Most of the buildings – government, commercial, residential – were from the nineteenth century. It gave the place a homey, relaxed feel – as if the flow of time had stopped in about 1845. It's a place, I thought, perfectly happy in its unchanging uniqueness. In a way it was like walking through the pages of one of

MT's novels. I half-expected to run into Tom and Huck on their way home from spending the day larking around on the river.

The following morning I was eating breakfast at the hotel and noticed the dining room was teeming with matronly women in thick suits; their jackets were festooned with what appeared to be medals. The decorations on these girls' bosoms would put the top brass of a banana republic to shame.

This was clearly a convention of some sort, so I decided to discover what these women were up to. Two of them were sitting at the next table, so I asked them; they were happy to enlighten me; and very cheerful and polite they were. These women were, in fact, members of an organization called Daughters of the American Revolution – DAR for short.

"So, do you hate the Brits these days... want to do away with the Monarchy and so on?" I asked with a wink.

"No, no, no," one said quite seriously, "we work to promote education, historic preservation and patriotism." She sounded a little like a parrot, but I liked these women, and respected their dedication to their country. These are women, they explained, who can trace their lineage back to the time of the Revolution and authenticate that their forebears fought on the right side.

Nowadays, I think one could safely predict they disapprove of the President and support the Second Amendment. It made me smile to think they all might have *derringers* in their purses. Many prominent women have belonged to the DAR: Susan B. Anthony, Mary Baker Eddy, Grandma Moses, Ginger Rogers, Laura Bush, Rosalynn Carter, and my personal favorite, Bo Derek.

In 1939, First Lady Eleanor Roosevelt renounced her membership in the DAR because it barred world-renown black contralto Marian Anderson from singing at their national convention in Washington.

With breakfast profitably concluded, I thought it might be interesting to take a ride on the Hannibal Trolley, a 14-mile circuit around the area, sure to disclose some of Hannibal's hidden gems. So I hoofed it to their office on North Main Street. It was a funny little place staffed by a rather worn-out couple who didn't seem to enjoy what they were doing – taking money and handing out tiny blue tickets. My ticket was so small I thought I might lose it before I had to board. There was scarcely room for the words *Admit One* printed on it.

There was a rather dormant-looking snack bar in the rear. The menu was scrawled on a chalkboard high on the wall; the feature item was a *Hot Dog*, or it might have been *Hotdog*, I'm not sure. The price was $1. Now I just love a good hotdog, and one for a dollar or less, drowned in mustard, is completely irresistible to me. I walked over to the machine that's supposed to cook them and keep them hot, but to my dismay I found it empty and cold. Moreover, the machine was so clean, I suspect the management hadn't cooked a 'dog there for months. These premises were, to borrow from Mr. Cleese, 'uncontaminated' with hotdogs of any kind.

No matter, it was time to get the tour on the road. Our driver was a good old boy with the odd nickname, Cotton. He was absolutely burgeoning with local lore, a ceaseless torrent spoken in a gorgeous Missouri drawl. His grammar was idiosyncratic and would have made my father, a rigorous grammarian, howl in disapproval and derision.

In any case, I listened intently, and got the gist of what he was saying, although I missed quite a bit. He clearly loved the area, loved his subject, and was very kind to his passengers. He talked about Mark Twain and his novels' characters as if they were neighbors of his, which, in a sense, they were. He assumed his audience was well-versed in Twain's work – which I doubt was true; but he did give us the benefit of the doubt.

The thing I most wanted to see in the area was the huge cave complex just east of town, the one named after – you guessed it – Mr. Twain. Missouri is riddled with limestone caves, over six thousand of them – but this one is world-famous. The young Mark Twain – then known by his real name, Sam Clemens – loved to explore the cave and fantasize about it.

In *The Adventures of Tom Sawyer,* it's known as McDougal's Cave.
*The cave was but a labyrinth of crooked aisles that ran
into each other and out again and led nowhere. It was
said that one might wander days and nights together
through its intricate tangle of rifts and chasms and
never find the end of the cave.*

On one occasion Tom and his girlfriend, Becky, got lost in the cave for several days. While there, Tom detected a third person in the cave; this was the villain of the story, Injun Joe, whom Twain depicted as *evil* personified. He was a wicked, cruel and cunning man – a thuggish murderer and grave-robber who'd been hiding from the law in the gloomy recesses of the cave. Clever Tom – with moribund Becky in tow – eventually emerged from the cave and they were later welcomed home with great joy.

Becky's father, Judge Thatcher, considered the cave a menace to the children of the town and – ignorant of Injun Joe's being inside – had the entrance sealed. Tom learned of this some days later and alerted authorities, who, after unsealing the cave, found Injun Joe – starved to death. Injun Joe is a thoroughly unsympathetic character in the novel, and his miserable end Twain meant to portray a just vengeance.

The Adventures of Tom Sawyer was published in 1876 and was a big international hit; many readers traveled to Hannibal – especially to see the cave. In 1886 tours were commenced and have been going ever since, making this the oldest continuously-operating 'show cave' in Missouri. It is a U.S. National Historic Landmark, and rightly so – it really is terrific, a veritable *maze* consisting of 260 passages, covering six miles.

Our guide was a slip of a girl named Alison, a freshman at Hannibal-Lagrange University. She was new in the job, very keen and polite. Early on in the tour she asked our group of about eight how we'd feel if she turned off all the lights. We were all pretty comfortable with that idea, so she did so. What followed was an experience that can scarcely be described.

An extraordinary darkness fell over us; it felt being swallowed up by a thick black velvet shroud. The darkness was palpable; it felt heavy and life-threatening, like being buried in soot. Whether you opened your eyes or closed them made no difference, which was a strange experience in itself. After thirty seconds I started experiencing thin streaks of light in my field of vision, no doubt arising from my optic nerves straining to see something, *anything*. It was a disconcerting and surprising sensation, totally unlike being in a darkened room. Shortly thereafter, mercifully, she switched the lights back on.

She remarked, "You know, if you were kept in total blackness for three days, you couldn't tell if you were awake or asleep."

I don't doubt it a bit. I'd be a gibbering idiot inside an hour. I began to think how miserable it would be to be trapped in a coal mine, with no light, no way out, no hope of rescue. This experience was truly a vision of Hell for me. The early tours by lamplight must have been spine-tingling. I asked Alison what we'd do in the event of a power outage, or an earthquake. She replied reassuringly, "I have two flashlights."

A series of macabre events took place in this cave that Alison omitted to mention; perhaps she didn't want to spook us. In the late 1840s a local physician named Joseph Nash McDowell, former anatomy instructor at Missouri Medical College, bought the cave for the purpose of conducting experiments on human cadavers. His most noteworthy activity involved the attempt to petrify the remains of his deceased daughter. In his non-fiction *Life on the Mississippi*, Twain had this to say about McDowell's work:

> *In my time the person who owned the cave turned it into*
> *a mausoleum for his daughter, age fourteen. The body*
> *of this poor child was put into a copper cylinder filled*

with alcohol, and this suspended in one of the dismal
avenues of the cave.

The girl's body was eventually forcibly removed by angry local residents who had learned of the situation from children who'd explored the cave and seen the goings-on. The townsfolk rather turned against Dr. McDowell after that, accusing him of a host of unholy offenses: grave-robbing and necrophilia among them. You know how people gossip.

Alison led us deeper into the cave. In the midst we came to a side-passage that was barred; nailed to the barrier was a crude sign: "Jesse James Hide-Out." It was news to me that Jesse James had anything to do with this cave. Naturally, I'd heard of James, but I didn't know much about him – just that he was a 19th century outlaw people refer to as if they'd liked to have known him – a splendid, dashing chap – a virtual Robin Hood figure.

The fact that he and I had been in the very same cave was somehow of great interest to me. I wondered how Jesse James happened to be associated with this particular cave. I discovered that Dr. McDowell was an ardent supporter of the Confederacy; he used his cave to stockpile weapons and ammunition for these soldiers. During the war McDowell met a young Confederate named Jesse James, and in the course of becoming acquainted, showed him the cave.

Incredibly, Jesse was only fourteen at the time, and was already a member of Quantrill's Rangers – a band of Confederate *bushwhackers* – notorious for their brutality against Unionists and abolitionists alike. The war years – that desperate, lawless, bloody, hopeless time – must have left a deep and incurable wound in the soul of Jesse James.

After the war was over, there wasn't much call for bushwhackers, so Jesse looked around to see what line of work might engage his imagination, while providing a comfortable living. His skills involved plunder, slaughter and imposing his will by force of arms, so he figured taking other people's money was an easier job than any other that occurred to him.

Jesse and his gang developed a special proficiency in knocking over banks, stagecoaches and trains. Their first bank job was in 1866 at the Clay County Savings Association in Liberty, Missouri. For history buffs, this was the first daytime robbery of an American bank in peacetime. Such daring acts led to his attaining a certain celebrity.

In 1879 the gang robbed a train south of Hannibal and headed to Dr. McDowell's cave and used it as a hide-out for several days. I asked myself, how can they possibly know this? The answer is simple: Jesse wrote his name in pencil on the wall of the cave, giving the date, which corresponds with the date of the robbery. I suppose an investigative reporter could challenge the authenticity of this finding, but the locals believe it, and it's certainly good for business. The reason that part of the cave is closed off is that Jesse's writing is becoming fainter with age, and the management doesn't want riff-raff tourists like me breathing on it.

It irritates me when a criminal attains celebrity status. I don't have much sympathy for the unrepentant criminal, who is, by definition, a psychopath of considerable degree. The characteristics of psychopathy include a deficient conscience, vanity, impulsiveness, aversion to responsibility, lack of empathy, and so on. What makes this condition truly malignant is that the psychopath – especially an intelligent one – is able to charm and deceive his victims. So, on that basis, I think Jesse James was a true psychopath. It's only through the lens of history that such a person seems *romantic*.

The most surprising thing I learned about Jesse James concerns his father, Robert Sallee James. He came from a distinguished English family that arrived in America two generations earlier. Jesse's middle name was Woodson, after his great-grandfather, Dr. John Woodson, an Oxford-trained surgeon.

As a young man, Robert was a gifted student who earned a Master of Arts degree and went on to be ordained a Baptist pastor. He was one of the founders of William Jewell College, a private liberal arts institution in Liberty, Missouri. This college is thriving to this day; its motto is *Deo Fisus Labora* – Trust God Work – which doesn't translate slickly for want of punctuation, but you get the idea.

Robert had a special interest in 'revival,' and felt called to preach to the men of the California gold rush. Sadly, he contracted cholera there, and died in 1850, at the age of 32. Jesse was three at the time, and the loss of his father undoubtedly played a role in his destiny. Perhaps he was angry at God.

Well, I surely got my money's worth at the Mark Twain Cave; it was a stimulating experience and great fun. In the late afternoon, Cotton swung by in the trolley with a new gang of passengers; I jumped on and rode happily back downtown to the little depot. All that spelunking had given me quite an appetite, so I decided to splurge for dinner. Accordingly, at the appointed time, I sauntered across the street to the Mark Twain Dinette. I ordered Mississippi River catfish, fries, salad and a beer, and returned to the hotel thinking, all in all, this had been a very good day. I felt like a comet that had just streaked through the universe according to Mark Twain.

I planned to move downriver the afternoon of the following day, so I spent the morning rambling around on foot. On the edge of town, at the top of a steep hill, is a park called *Lovers' Leap*. From this high point, so the story goes, two Indian lovers from warring tribes jumped to their deaths, rather than part. It's a variation on the eternal *Romeo and Juliet* story. I was expecting a dizzying cliff, but it was modest indeed – and honestly – unless you took a headlong dive off it, you might escape with scrapes and bruises. I found the whole place pretty unconvincing, but climbing the hill was invigorating, and the wide view of the river made my heart sing.

Being a peripatetic lad, I decided to walk downtown for one last fond look at Hannibal and the river. The day before, Cotton had pointed out a certain handsome building on the street grandly called 'Broadway.' The style of the building was fantastically out-of-place: its architecture was typical Greek Neoclassical, with four mighty grey concrete Ionian columns supporting the roof. Seriously, it looks like a junior version of the New York Stock Exchange. Carved into the concrete of the gable was the date – 1830 – and the company name, *Farmers & Merchants Bank.* I noted there was not an apostrophe in sight – a shame in a town with such a literary heritage.

The building was remarkable in its own right for its utter eccentricity, but Cotton embarked on what I later learned was a major embellishment of the facts – an improvement on the truth, as Mr. Twain might have said. Cotton, that dear old Hannibal-booster, told us that this place was robbed in the thirties by the infamous John Dillinger, the very *king* of bank robbers – another bloody celebrity crook. Well, of course I believed every word, but upon doing a little research, I discovered an imaginative reworking of the facts. First, Dillinger never robbed a single bank in Missouri; secondly, this Farmers & Merchants Bank had *never* been robbed in its history – though I'll bet it crossed Jesse James's mind to give it a try. Poor old Cotton was doubtless just passing on misinformation he acquired years ago – but he's such a fine fellow, I'll let somebody else set him straight.

My trip was rapidly coming to a close, but I wanted to gain some insight into what kind of a man Mark Twain was, and what he really believed about his life and work. He'd have certainly have made a stimulating seat-mate on the bus. He was tremendously prolific and his aphorisms appear all over town, mugs, plaques, postcards, T-shirts. Purely subjectively, let me present some of what are to me, his most self-revelatory quotations.

First, we must remember that he was principally a *satirist*; his aim and method were to point out human folly – holding it up to scorn with the idea of getting a laugh. This of course involves the liberal use of sarcasm; he was very good at it, too; there was certainly no shortage of material to work with.

Ah, sarcasm – I've thought a good deal about it, and as I get older, I'm gaining an understanding of its nature, its essential unkindness, even cruelty: getting a laugh at the expense of another. I briefly touched on sarcasm in "The Road to Key West."

The word itself is from the Greek *sarkasmos*, meaning *sneer;* it also suggests the *tearing off of flesh.* Some cultures – certainly the British – liberally use sarcasm in their humor; it's really the basis of British humor. Sarcasm been called the *lowest* form of humor by Oscar Wilde – and the *highest* by Basil Fawlty. Whichever it is – low or high – it's a sharp instrument, leaving the ground covered in chunks of bloody flesh, as it were.

Some – like myself – can't seem to help using sarcasm; I wish I could. I agree with Thomas Carlyle's view: "Sarcasm I now see to be, in general, the language of the Devil; for which reason I have, long since, as good as renounced it." Such renunciation for me, I fear, would require Trappist vows. But I do live in hope.

The history of satirical writing is long indeed, stretching from Aesop, through Chaucer, Shakespeare and Dickens, up to Woody Allen, Gary Larson and Bill Maher. The best of the satirists – say, Jonathan Swift – hope to improve society with their work, and Twain at his best seems to have had the same aim; he castigated racism, imperialism and greed. He could be uproariously funny, and toured the country giving amusing speeches – much like a stand-up comic of today. Much of his material, though, I find caustic, insulting and even oddly unsophisticated.

To be fair, let me give you a sampling of the man's writing in his various moods, ranging from the light and kindly, to the dark and bitter:

- Nothing so liberates a man and expands the kindly instincts that nature put in him as travel and contact with many kinds of people.

- Kindness is the language which the deaf can hear and the blind can see.
- The difference between the right word and the almost right word word is the difference between lightning and a lightning bug.
- There are rest and healing in the contemplation of antiquities.
- The universal brotherhood of man is our most precious possession.
- Don't worry about the lines on your face, they merely indicate where the smiles have been.
- The man who does not read good books has no advantage over the man who can't read them.
- The Jews have the best average brain in the world... they are the world's intellectual aristocracy.

He thought the German language was "awful." Because, he says, "a young lady has no sex, but a turnip has... and that nouns are not *words*, but *alphabetical processions*... the language needs to be trimmed down and repaired."

- Everything human is pathetic. The secret source of Humor itself is not joy but sorrow. There is no humor in Heaven.
- Sanity and happiness are an impossible combination.
- There is no distinctly native American criminal class except Congress.
- Suppose you were an idiot, and suppose you were a member of Congress. But I repeat myself.

About his landlady in Italy: "a reptile with a filthy soul."

About his business partner James Paige: "If I had his nuts in a steel-trap I would... watch the trap till he died."

- Man is the only creature that kills for fun... he is the only creature that has a nasty mind.
- Go to Heaven for the climate, Hell for the company.
- Man is a marvelous curiosity. When he is at his very, very best,

he is a sort of low grade nickel-plated angel... all the time he is a sarcasm.

In a letter to his wife, Livi, in 1889: "I believe I am superior to the God of the Bible."

It is quite obvious from Twain's writing, including his autobiography, that as he grew older, he became increasingly unhappy. I believe this must be the natural history of the professional satirist. Twain was not only a satirist, but an acknowledged *narcissist*. His unhappiness was compounded by what I'd call his lack of *spiritual resources* upon which to draw. A nominal Presbyterian, his religious views, were, in the context of his time, bizarre, and often blasphemous.

His daughter Clara noted that the main reason he never attended church was that "he couldn't bear to hear anyone but himself talk." He was also a Freemason and member of the Society for Psychical Research, which could do nothing but muddy his religious views. In *Mark Twain's Notebook* (1894), he wrote that if there's one kind of person Jesus would not be, it would be a Christian. This to me is senseless, but I'd love to have asked him the reason for his hostility. It must have been personal.

Twain's sadness deepened when his daughter Susy died in 1896 at age 24. This was followed by the death of his beloved wife Olivia in 1904 at age 58, and his daughter Jean in 1909 at age 29. He was also under chronic financial strain because of a series of disastrous investments. He railed against Wall Street, and the growing American empire its capital funded. "I am opposed to millionaires," he noted, "but it would be dangerous to offer me the position."

His last book, *Letters from the Earth* (1909), was highly controversial; Clara kept it from publication until 1962 because of its savage contempt for God, Christ and Man. The 'Letters,' by the way, were written by 'the Archangel Satan' on Earth to the other Archangels Gabriel and Michael in Heaven.

Clara, it is of interest to note, was a Christian Scientist, something that would have made her father fairly spin in his grave.

The book of Proverbs tells us that *as a man thinks, so he is*. In his 1903 classic *As a Man Thinketh*, American author James Allen agrees: *The sum of a man's thoughts are his character. His character influences the conditions and circumstances of his life.* So, very sadly, Mark Twain – this genius wit, this giant of world literature – in the end reaped from his own soul what he had sown there – something very bitter and hopeless.

When my father was old, he had a printed prayer on his desk. It was a plea that in his final years he would be a person other people liked to be around. It ended with words I've never forgotten: *a sour old person is one of the crowning works of the devil.* In this respect, I think Mark Twain rather outsmarted himself. My father's prayer, by the way, was granted splendidly.

In any case, based on my limited survey of Mark Twain, I arrived at the opinion that anyone who thinks he's better than God and recommends the 'company' in Hell would likely not have much to stir me, no matter how witty or erudite. I realize Twain is venerated in most quarters, but I can't bring myself to subscribe, for the reasons outlined above. It's interesting to note he was very popular with the old Soviet regime, for what I believe are obvious reasons.

I was getting a bit tired of the solitude and egregious diet; suddenly I felt I'd been away from home for long enough; I felt like I'd pretty much run out of gas. So I booked a flight out of St. Louis, a hundred miles south of Hannibal. I'd bought a bus ticket on-line; it said I had to print it out for the driver, but the hotel printer was on the blink. I figured, I'd just give the driver my confirmation number, and all would be well.

I needed to get back to the Arby's on Route 61, so I gave Huck's a call – there's just no escaping Mark Twain in this town. The same driver – maybe it was Huck himself – in the same jalopy came to pick me up. There was another fellow aboard; I wasn't sure where he fit in, and the driver didn't introduce us. Maybe, I thought, he was 'riding shotgun.'

We rode along through downtown, while the other passenger, whom I'll call Billy-Bob, prattled about how unsatisfactory things are in this area nowadays. He's a local fellow, in his late forties. When he gets bored with Hannibal he goes to Philadelphia to get his belly-full city living. We were crossing Broadway when he looked to his right and said, "Looka Broadway… nuttin' goin' on there, notta thing…. pah-thetic. Reckon ah'll g'back t' Philly purdy soon."

Well, we drove for about half an hour and I was beginning to think I'd been kidnapped. In any case, I was getting worried about catching my bus. I spoke up, "Say, how much longer till we get to Arby's on Route 61?" The driver mumbled something about having to take Billy-Bob to work for the four o'clock shift at the General Mills plant – which I knew was on the other edge of town from my destination.

Another ten minutes passed. Finally we rolled through the gate of a very smart-looking factory. I asked Billy-Bob what the plant produced; this seemed like a reasonable question to me, not too nosy.

He hesitated, and said, "Ah… let's see… we used to make Hamburger Helper, but we don't no more." He thought some more. "Progresso Soup, yup, we make Progresso Soup." In a factory that size they must make oceans of it.

This plant was built in 1972 by the William Underwood Company of Boston. You likely know its main product, Underwood's Deviled Ham – a tangy blend of ham, spices and mustard. Mr. Underwood wanted to build a plant close to the major hog farms of the nation; he decided on Missouri. As the story goes, he chose Hannibal because of his respect for Mark Twain and his wish to do something nice for the townspeople. General Mills took over the plant at a later date, but continued to produce the ham under the original brand.

Underwood's Deviled Ham comes in tiny cans meticulously

wrapped in white paper – with the charming logo of the devil on it. This is the oldest corporate logo in the country, some say almost as old as Old Scratch himself. How did they come up with that one? No one seems to know.

For decades, management awarded a jacket – complete with logo – to any employee who'd had a year's perfect attendance. It's said these jackets created something of a stir in local churches. To this day, one of the mottos associated with this product is *Better the devil you know.* The address of the General Mills plant? I jumped with surprise when I learned it: *1 Devil Road.* It seems to me the devil's had a free hand in Hannibal for ages.

Well, we dropped Billy-Bob off in time for work and set out for Arby's. Eventually we got there, and in plenty of time, too. The bill was $3.75, a minuscule fare for such a long ride.

So, I sat down in the restaurant and kept a sharp eye out for the arrival of the Trailways bus to St. Louis. One of the employees, a pleasant looking matronly woman seemed to be particularly welcoming, and I noticed she kept sweeping the floor just to my right side. I wondered if she wanted to talk.

"Are you a local lady?" I asked.

"Why, yes, I am, sir. Where are you from?"

I explained where I was from, that I was exploring the Mississippi Valley, and that I had thoroughly enjoyed my time in Hannibal.

"The best part about my job," she explained, "is that you meet folks from all over... all over the world. In fact, just this morning a man came in here from... Lith-u-ania."

She drifted away with her broom, but was soon back to within speaking range. There was something in her gaze that made me think she wanted to broach a certain subject. I took a guess.

"Are you religious?" I asked.

"Yes," she said, "I certainly am. I'm one of *Jehovah's Witnesses.*" She slipped me a glossy card inviting me to visit their website. I respected this woman for her polite approach; I slipped the card into my shirt pocket.

The bus eventually arrived – a big, red Trailways beauty – half an hour late. I didn't know it, but I was about to have my only unpleasant human exchange in any of the trips described in this book. I almost decided not to include it, but it was significant, and it upset me.

The door of the waiting bus was closed. The driver saw me approach with my two bags; I beat on the door; he opened it. "Can I stow my bags below?" I asked.

"No, just carry them aboard," he said curtly.

Well, I thought, this guy isn't exactly into *service.*

"Have a ticket?" he asked.

You will remember that my hotel's printer was down, but I did have an e-ticket on my phone.

"I have an e-ticket," I said with a degree of misgiving.

"No good." Our eyes met; it was like steel striking flint; I fancied a few sparks flew. "You gotta have a paper ticket."

I began to explain that I simply couldn't print a paper ticket because of a glitch at my hotel, but he wasn't having any of it.

"That's not my problem – it's yours. I don't have to let you on, you know." He stuck out his chin.

"Well," I said, "How do you want to play this?"

An age passed.

"Let's see your e-ticket," he snapped.

I handed over my phone.

"Gawd, what a small screen," he griped. Then he got down to business; he phoned HQ and confirmed my confirmation number – that's what they're for, after all. After much remonstrating, the decision was made: he would, under protest, let me on.

"If you try that stunt next time, I won't let you on," he warned.

I thought, "Fat chance I'll ever get on *your* flippin' bus again." If there is a 'next time' I'll get Huck's to take me to the airport; it would probably be cheaper, and certainly less annoying. I started toward my seat.

"I hope I haven't ruined your *whole* day," said I, trying not to sound too snarky.

"It's not about *my* day," snipped the bus-nazi. "It's about *you* delaying all the other passengers."

As far as I was concerned, it was *he* that was doing the delaying, and I told him so. At that, we declared a stand-off. I was still pretty huffy, but I took a seat, tried to lower my blood pressure and erase the experience from my mind.

(Upon reflection, his crankiness reminded me of a patient of mine long ago. Jim was a bus driver who lost his temper one day while driving his regular route through the city. He suddenly got fed-up with the stresses of the day, and simply parked his bus – with passengers – and simply walked home. He turned out to have an inoperable brain tumor. So… you never know.)

A couple of hours passed; then something rather unexpected happened. We were heading for the bus stop at Lambert-St. Louis International Airport; I had booked a hotel nearby for that night and planned to fly home the following morning. I don't think the driver was expecting anyone to be getting off, but he stopped anyway. I gathered my things and started for the front door; I could see him eying me in the mirror as I came up the aisle; I felt like boxing his right ear as I went by – a little something to remember me by.

I was going to alight without a word, but he called out, "Hey, young man – oh, is *this* your stop? Do you have all your personal belongings? Have a great day!"

I was pretty shocked at his change in attitude and I squeezed out a "thank you" with my teeth clenched.

I have two thoughts on that turn of events. First is that precious-few bus passengers are in a position to be *flying* anywhere; secondly, perhaps he suspected I was an undercover bus-inspector who might be assigning him a failing grade – so he'd better make a last-ditch attempt to redeem himself.

I can't tell you how glad I am that most bus drivers are easier to deal with than this bozo. Most are rather business-like, while others act like prison guards. My favorites are, of course, the friendly and helpful kind – like the cheery folks who work as greeters at Wal-mart.

Well, here I was at the Lambert-St. Louis International Airport – what do you know? This is no *ordinary* airport; its history is amazing and illustrious. It is named after Albert Bond Lambert (1875–1946) who was a very interesting fellow; he contributed immeasurably to both the city of St. Louis and the world of aviation.

He was born in St. Louis, into the founding family of Lambert Pharmacal, inventors of that staple of the bathroom, *Listerine*. He became company president in 1896. Apparently that job didn't absorb all his energy; he became an accomplished golfer and made the U.S. Olympic golf team that subsequently won the silver medal in Paris in 1904. One imagines he had money to burn.

Lambert developed an interest in, of all things, *flying* – not exactly a popular pursuit at the time. In 1909 he met the Wright brothers, and subsequently purchased his first airplane from them. Orville Wright himself gave Lambert flying lessons, and in 1911 he became the first St. Louis resident to earn a pilot's license.

Lambert was a true visionary with the drive, money and time to pursue his dreams. In 1925 he bought a 170-acre field northwest of St. Louis – a place normally used by hot-air balloonists. He set to work building a proper 'airport' – a new concept at the time. Over the next seven years, at his own expense, he constructed numerous runways and hangars. Around this time, Lambert met fellow-aviator Charles Lindbergh. At that time Lindbergh was a university drop-out who flew mail between Chicago and St. Louis. The friendship between Lambert and Lindbergh proved to be of great historic significance.

In 1919, wealthy French-born New York hotelier Raymond Orteig had offered $25,000 to the first pilot to fly across the Atlantic. Several aviators died in the attempt. However, by 1924 aviation had come a long way; Lambert, Lindbergh and some well-heeled friends decided to form a committee to take up the challenge. They developed a single-engine, single-seat, cloth-covered high-wing monoplane with a fuel capacity of 450 gallons. The name of the engine was the *Wright Whirlwind,* which I think is wonderful. No wonder it succeeded.

On May 20, 1927 the *Spirit of St. Louis* took off from Garden City, Long Island, New York, and after 33 hours of nearly unendurable suspense, landed neatly at Aeroport LeBourget in Paris. Lindbergh's journey was a stunning achievement, of course; what is lesser known is that his anticipated arrival caused the biggest traffic jam in French history – which gives you an idea how the feat captured the public imagination.

The next year, Lambert sold his little airport to the City of St. Louis for $68,000 – the same price he paid for it, before all the work. This land is where Lambert–St. Louis International Airport sits today. Albert Lambert established what later became the first municipal airport in the country, which rather points out the power of an energetic, smart dreamer. The terminal building, incidentally, was designed by architect Minoru Yamasaki who also designed the World Trade Center. The terminal design inspired those at John F. Kennedy International Airport in New York and l'aéroport Paris-Charles de Gaulle.

The next morning I caught my flight for home. Originally, I had hoped to follow the Mississippi from its headwaters in Minnesota all the way to the Gulf, over two thousand miles. When I began to plan this trip, I consulted my dog-eared companion, the *Rand McNally Road Atlas.* It looked to me as though it would be an easy downhill run, rather like coasting. I thought of it in terms of basic physics; all I was doing was, like the river itself, cooperating with gravity. Looked at another way, I thought I'd be simply rolling downhill, from north to south, in conformity with the curvature of the Earth – rather like a teardrop of joy rolling down a cheek. I reckoned ten – maybe fourteen – days would do it.

I don't know how many times I have to learn the same lesson: that running my finger over a map is a poor way to estimate the time and effort involved in completing a journey. This won't surprise you – but to me a trip is a splendid excuse for getting out into the wide world, to see what's to be seen, and learn what's to be learned. A journey is a stimulus for thought – a way to enlarge one's view of life and stock of ideas, to confirm or refute one's assumptions, to develop and burnish one's philosophy.

My old friend, Steinbeck, said this about the difference between one's plans and the journey itself: "… schedules, reservations brass-bound and inevitable, dash themselves to wreckage on the personality of the trip." I love that. Mercifully, there wasn't much wreckage associated with this one, but I had indeed fallen far short of my goal. In my heart though, my aim was to sample the river and its life, and in that I am well-satisfied. Besides, I now I have an excuse for another trip. The southern half of the River beckons – and it's *bound* to be thrilling.

Thanks for traveling with me. I hope you've enjoyed the ride. See you down the road.

ABOUT THE AUTHOR

Dr. Trevor Watson's insatiable curiosity and itchy feet have led him to travel and work in many parts of the world. He has practised medicine for over 40 years, and has a keen interest in psychology, philosophy and spirituality. He and his wife, Cynthia, have been married for 46 marvellous years. He has two children and four grandchildren. Allowing for sensible buffer-zones, they all live near one another on Vancouver Island, BC.

27056080R00122

Printed in Great Britain
by Amazon